Organization Theories and Public Administration

Charles R. Davis

PRAEGER

Westport, Connecticut
London

Library of Congress Cataloging-in-Publication Data

Davis, Charles R.
    Organization theories and public administration / Charles R.
Davis.
        p.   cm.
    Includes bibliographical references and index.
    ISBN 0-275-95576-1 (alk. paper)
    1. Public administration. 2. Organizational theory. I. Title.
JF1351.D38   1996
350—dc20   95-53000

British Library Cataloguing in Publication Data is available.

Library of Congress Catalog Card Number: 95-53000
ISBN: 0-275-95576-1

First published in 1996

Praeger Publishers, 88 Post Road West, Westport, CT 06881
An imprint of Greenwood Publishing Group, Inc.

Printed in the United States of America

The paper used in this book complies with the
Permanent Paper Standard issued by the National
Information Standards Organization (Z39.48-1984).

10 9 8 7 6 5 4 3 2 1

Organization Theories and Public Administration

To Raymonda Carolyn Davis

Contents

Preface

Political theory has long accepted as axiomatic that values inform human actions. Likewise, everyday administrative practices in government have been intensely influenced by various organizational theories put forth over the past century. Indeed, many theories have been advanced within this time span, and many prominent organizational perspectives have been applied to government sector enterprises. Among these are those of Woodrow Wilson, Frank Goodnow, Max Weber, Frederick Winslow Taylor, Luther Gulick, Dwight Waldo, Chester Bernard, Herbert Simon, Robert Golembiewski, Ralph Hummel, Michael Harmon, Robert Denhardt, and other academic writers. Obviously these scholars constitute a prominent but only partial listing of individuals who, in the literature of public administration, have contributed to the theory and practice of American governmental administration and organizations.

Therefore, numerous organizational perspectives have informed the practices and actions of governmental organizations. Yet the determination of which model, if any, possesses the capability of promoting authentic "public" organizational existence for its human composition is an unsettled matter. It is, indeed, very much an open issue. This book examines four prevalent perspectives of organization and proposes criteria for consideration in an alternative theory for more genuinely public organizational life. In short, this book is conceived as an exercise in political theory applied to different organizational models.

Acknowledgments

Several individuals have been instrumental in the support and development of this project.

First, a word of special appreciation should go to the scholars who have guided and particularly influenced my own development in political theory and organizations. Foremost among these are Herbert G. Reid and Ernest Yanarella at the University of Kentucky. Also, I would like to express my gratitude to Dave Lowery at the University of North Carolina at Chapel Hill who introduced me to the study of the behavior and politics of public administration. For his scholarly influence, over several years, on my thinking about public organization, I also thank Robert B. Denhardt of the University of Delaware. Larry Busch of Michigan State and Lee Sigelman of George Washington University also warrant my acknowledgement for their help in focusing my thinking and writing in two of the chapters which originally appeared elsewhere.

Thanks should likewise go to my colleagues in the Department of Political Science at the University of Southern Mississippi. My appreciation is extended particularly to Ron Marquardt for his encouragement.

The insights gained through my experience in federal and state governmental settings contributed in several ways to the development of this project. The two people I would most like to thank in this regard are those persons who hired and directed me in applied policy and evaluation research. They are Chris Conover who is presently at Duke's Center for Health Policy Studies and Chuck Gollmar with the Centers for Disease Control in Atlanta.

For her generous time and effort in converting files and for her other areas of computer expertise, thanks also goes to my sister LaVada Davis.

Organization
Theories and Public
Administration

Introduction

The identification of government organizations as "public" organizations in American society is an everyday occurrence. While this understanding has some plausible application to government bureaucracy's *external* relationships with other political institutions, it has little, if any, application *internally* to government organization itself. Indeed, frequently citizens erroneously equate government bureaucracy with public organization. This misunderstanding is found at all levels of society. It perpetuates the fiction that "public" and "government" organizations are synonymous.

Before exploring various theories of organization and examining their prospects as authentic public organizational models, a discussion of the substantive variations between basic dimensions of "government" versus "public" organizations is warranted.

In examining modern American political society, government organizations are fundamentally instruments of state power. In other words, government organizations (more aptly, government bureaucracies) reside at the center of political power in the contemporary liberal-administrative state.[1] Put simply, the modern state is ultimately concerned with the centrality of political power in everyday life.

Frequently, among the mass media, and therefore among the general population, government bureaucracies in the United States are designated as "public" entities (typically referred to as public administration). There are at least two reasons for such designations: since these bureaucracies are simply attached to government (and as government is seen as equivalent to public), such organizations are labeled "public"; and both academics and the general populace habitually, but often erroneously, label government entities as public organizations simply to distinguish such organizations from corporate or private sector enterprises.

Several very fundamental differences exist between public and government organizations. While government organizations are primarily apparatuses of state power, these types of organization can indeed be democratic or quasi-democratic. However, they can just as equally be authoritarian (externally, as they are frequently internally). Likewise, as Weber knew only too well, these bureaucracies can and do serve any type of state power structure or leadership.

For instance, consider the government organizations of Hitler's Third Reich, Franco's Spain, Stalin's Russia, or Peron's Argentina. The bureaucratic apparatuses in all these were government instruments of state power, but none of these remotely qualified as "public" as the term has been used during the more than 2500 years of democratic thought.

In order to formulate a more authentic public organization theory, it is necessary to examine more closely the differences between public and government types of enterprises. Specifically, this is needed in order to develop a theory of organization that can genuinely facilitate an enterprise based in public values and practices.

As noted above, in American political society, government organizations are typically designated as public entities. However, this statement merits truth only in very confining circumstances, namely, applying the term *public* to the external aspects of political bureaucracy. More aptly, government bureaucracies are instruments of the contemporary liberal state, but, internally American government bureaucracy does not qualify as "public" according to either traditional or modern democratic thought. Indeed, in organizational structure, democracy and bureaucracy are opposites of each other.

In other words, the most significant *political* characteristic of modern government organization is the prevalent structure by which these enterprises are organized at the federal, state, and local levels. Specifically, this is by administrative bureaucracy, which dominates most forms of government organization in the United States. Since the late nineteenth century, American government organizations,[2] particularly at the national level, have been, for nearly a hundred years now, increasingly top-down bureaucratic apparatuses undergirded by calculative means-ends rationality.[3]

This dominant characteristic of government organization can readily be contrasted to characteristics of the public as traditionally associated with democratic political theory. The concept of *the public* found its initial expression in Greek and Roman Republic political thought. Aristotle gives the public its early definition as the "common involvement" of "man as a political animal." So the public constituted the common association of the combined citizenry of the Greek *polis*.[4] This was true obviously for Athens, but it also held for militaristic Sparta and others as well. These city-states were established by collaborative efforts where "individualism was . . . tolerated for its contribution to the city's strength." Yet it was an ultimate "commitment to politics" (i.e., *shared* decision making) that primarily constituted the "good life."[5]

In both the Greek model and that of the Roman Republic, the idea of the state and politics was intimately tied to the common collaboration of citizens. Indeed, in the Greek model, the public or the state was synonymous with the whole political community of citizens. Yet the common union or state could be characterized as such only to the extent that all its citizens had the ability to share in the power of the polis (i.e., only as long as meaningful participation by each citizen was possible). A citizen, consequently, was one who participated in the legislative and judicial deliberations of the democratic, common association. Furthermore, a citizen's claim for substantive policymaking or participation "flowed," according to Sheldon Wolin, "from his contribution to the true end" of the state which was the person's involvement in the "civilized life of the community."[6]

Aristotle's description of the public association was interdependently related to the politics of citizenship, or, as Wolin points out, this involved active participation in policymaking. This is so because the notion of citizenship itself included the right of the individual to live in the only form of association that allowed one to develop one's capacities to the fullest. Therefore, in this sense, citizen participation in the public association was a claim flowing directly from the nature of man himself as a political animal.[7] In Aristotle's view, there is a "natural impulse" toward citizen participation in the common or public good because "man is the best of all animals when he has reached his full development.[8] Thus "full development" directly entails political participation in the policymaking agenda of the common organization or association of shared life.

Not only is citizenship and the state in antiquity tied to the public, but also the idea of the public was directly connected to the idea of the political in classical political thought. Indeed, *the common, the general,* and *the public* have a long history of use as equivalent expressions for what is political.[9] Moreover, the public involved that which concerned the state.[10] Plato, also, "displayed a sure sense" that the political has to do with "what is public in the life of society."[11]

Centuries later under the Roman Republic, Cicero, too, maintained the connection between the public and the political in everyday existence. It was this relationship that Cicero had in mind when he called the "commonwealth a *res publica,* a public thing, or the property of the people."[12]

Substantial changes have obviously transpired in the notion of the state since the last days of the Roman Republic. Likewise, the concept of the public has undergone changes while remaining true in some ways to original intentions.

For example, modern scholars such as Jurgen Habermas and John Dewey, in particular, are quite lucid in illuminating the transformation of the public since antiquity. Habermas is also quite helpful in presenting a brief history of the public over recent centuries.

According to Habermas, there is nothing to indicate that European society of the high Middle Ages ever possessed a distinct public realm of human existence separate from a distinctively private body of human activity. Indeed, Habermas' works describe the emergence of the public or public sphere of human activity as a development that occurred late in the history of Europe.[13]

The public sphere was a realm or body of bourgeois culture and came into full-blown existence between the seventeenth and twentieth centuries. It arose as a social category from medieval feudalism as liberal economic individualism emancipated itself from the absolutist state.[14]

Habermas says that the public sphere was first of all a realm of human social life where something approaching public opinion could be formed. Furthermore, the function of this public realm was to allow all citizens access to an atmosphere free of restriction or coercion by any other form of authority. Thus, in this public sphere, rational discussion and debate on problems of common concern could be addressed by the citizens.[15]

While the public sphere and classical public share an intent toward the participation in the common good, the public sphere does not correspond to the relationship found between the state and society in antiquity. That is, in early industrial society, the public sphere mediated between society and the state. By the late eighteenth century, the public had become a liberal institution within constitutionalist states originating out of the exchange economies of western nations. This situation occurred through the transformation of political power of capitalism and constitutional governments. In these new states the public realm came to be a mediating body between society (which was now essentially a realm of private autonomy) and the state. However, over time and through continual interweaving and diffusion of the state with the social sectors, the public sphere came to be "delimited in its widespread feasibility."[16] It is delimited because the modern liberal state has refeudalized the public realm. Thus today political authorities assume certain functions in the sphere of social labor and commodity exchange. Conversely, social powers, Habermas says, assume political functions. Additionally, large organizations work for political compromise with the state and with each other, avoiding the public sphere where possible.

John Dewey's approach to the public is more universal and less historical than Habermas' work. Yet both Dewey and Habermas converge in their analysis of what constitutes the essential dimensions of the public. Specifically, both share a similar orientation toward public attributes and action.

The idea of the public is first analyzed by Dewey as grounded in conjoint human activity and the lasting and serious consequences of such activity. According to Dewey, the public requires democracy that is not utopian but that "starts from the community as a fact." This, he points out, is the neighborly community or the "local as the ultimate universal."[17] In other words, the public in Dewey's work, at the local or community level requires social intelligence and the public's knowledge and awareness of itself.

Dewey and Habermas both therefore characterize the public in ways compatible with classical perspectives and with each other. That is, both scholars fundamentally identify the public as "expression" (Habermas) or "communication" (Dewey) of common interests arrived

at by free and open "discussion, debate and persuasion."[18] Specifically, Dewey, like Habermas, understood the public as providing for
the determination of common goals or a common agenda that could
be achieved only in a public enterprise. This public enterprise, association, community, or organization thus required open, mutual deliberation by participants affected by those goals. Alternately, the public represents only that which could be arrived at by expression of the
member participants of the human organization seeking the common
good.

   Dewey, writing in the late 1920s, and Habermas' more contemporary works both recognized the damaging impact of the liberal-
administrative state on diffusing the public sphere. In short, American public administration or government bureaucracies have, since the
early years of the century, posed a formidable barrier to any public's
awareness and knowledge of itself. This is because bureaucracies' first
commitment is to serving an oligarchy, economic class, or expertise,
what Dewey called the "captains of consciousness," the "captains of
industry," or what today is designated as the modern liberal-administrative state.

MODERN ORGANIZATIONAL THEORY AND
PRACTICE IN GOVERNMENT

   A fundamental principle of traditional western political theory that
was noted earlier is that theory always informs practice or values inform actions. This is universally true unless ideology intervenes to
conceal the true theory. It is the central thrust of this book to inquire
as to whether theories of organization found in American public administration qualify as authentic models of "public" organization. Do
these prevalent organizational approaches facilitate true public organizations? Consequently, a basic assumption made in evaluating these
organizational perspectives focuses on the theory-practice continuum.
The specific task here is to assess different organizational approaches
critically by inquiring as to whether varying theories generate authentic public action informed by genuine public values. Conversely, if
basic organizational practices, originating from a particular theory, are
informed by other than public values, then what are the real priorities
of such a theory? Moreover, why do such values take precedence over

public, democratic theory and practice?

The overriding concern in the following chapters is twofold. First, attention is directed toward illuminating the value priorities within and among various organizational theories that currently inform the thought and actions of human participants. Second, a critical analytical approach is employed to illuminate how and why different theories' primary values are *not* democratic and thus are *not* viable prospects for promoting actions that can legitimately be deemed "public" actions.

Chapters 1 through 4 examine basic value priorities of four prominent organizational theories. These concepts include: "efficiency," "rationality," "democratic administration," and "self-development." There are two purposes to examining these concerns critically across four organizational models. The first objective is understanding. Specifically, I endeavor to: (1) understand the meanings particular value priorities take and how these meanings have been transformed over time; (2) comprehend conflict within and across paradigms of organization in reference to broader social values; and (3) grasp implications of the hierarchy of priorities in each model, that is, those perspectives that predominate or are emphasized at the expense of other priorities.

The second objective is to provide insight into the considerations bearing on value and practice for reconstructing a critical theory of public organization. In its most basic aspects, a critical model is one fundamentally concerned with increasing democratic, as well as developmental, workplace potentialities for people who are affected by (and those who affect) decisions of the organization. Therefore, the basic thrust of this book is to assess the extent to which four distinct types of organizational models actually reflect public, democratic commitments and their practice in everyday work life.

THE ORGANIZATIONAL MODELS TO EXAMINE

There are four prevalent theories of organization selected for examination. These organizational paradigms are: (1) the monocentric model found in the writings of Luther Gulick; (2) the rational theory of organization put forth in Herbert Simon's writings; (3) the model of democratic administration formulated by Vincent Ostrom; and (4) the self-development paradigm expressed in the works of Chris Argyris. These four perspectives were chosen from among numerous organizational theories because each reflects one of four major subdisciplinary traditions in the literature of public administration. Furthermore, each writer generally exemplifies the thought represented in each of these four subschools of public administration. The specific traditions each theorist represents are: (1) the neo-orthodox approach typified by Luther Gulick; (2) the rational perspective symbolized by Herbert Simon; (3) the public policy orientation, of which Vincent Ostrom's public choice approach is a major expression; and (4) the self-development approach prominently found in the writings of Chris Argyris.

The perspectives of these four scholars can be briefly previewed by examining the variations in the structure of authority found in each theory. For instance, Gulick's monocentric model is characterized by one center of authority, although it is not based on a perfect hierarchy. By contrast, authority in Simon's theory centers on managerial rationality in accomplishing organizational objectives efficiently and particularly on the limited rationality in individual decision making. Ostrom's paradigm features a polycentric organizational arrangement with fragmentation and overlap of authority for enhanced individual opportunities. Finally, in the self-development perspective of Chris Argyris, one finds the structure of authority essentially identified as that found existing formally in organizations as systems. In other words, the self-development orientation to organization seeks to enhance personal and organizational health and well-being while accepting existing management authority structure.

APPROACHING ORGANIZATIONS CRITICALLY

It should be emphasized that this is a critical undertaking. My intent is not merely to assess the inadequate foundation of various theoretical perspectives for public organization but also to illuminate how and why the concerns for efficiency, rationality, self-interest, and self-development assume the priority they do, to the neglect and subordination of the commitments to public and democracy.

This effort therefore requires critically interpreting how historical and theoretical developments in the literature of Gulick, Simon,

Ostrom, and Argyris are influenced by the dialectical social totality in ways these theorists fail to recognize or only dimly perceive. By "dialectical social totality" is meant two reciprocal levels of influence on their thinking. First, this includes the historically specific cultural and ideological influences on each scholar's theoretical perspective. Second, it includes the influence on each theorist's writing on organization from each writer's respective place in the structure of political economy.

These influences will be approached in the following manner. For each analytic chapter, the historically specific settings are analyzed in terms of the implications posed by these settings upon their respective organizational model. In addition, each of these four analytic chapters critically examines the place of Gulick, Simon, Ostrom, and Argyris in the dynamic of political economy. These two tasks therefore entail interpreting critically the ramifications of possessive individualism and the modern corporate state. Such ramifications will be shown to contribute to a depoliticized and depublicized value emphasis in all four models of organizations.

TOWARD A MORE CRITICAL MODEL

Subsequent to Chapters 1 through 4, Chapter 5 elucidates the fact that each of the models examined in the first four chapters pose problems for public organization theory. Thus the goal in Chapter 5 is to search for, and try to outline, foundation considerations that more fully warrant the designation of "public" organization. This sketch in Chapter 5 places high priority on the organization itself for the realization of human needs by democratic politics. Moreover, it is demonstrated that meeting such needs politically includes not only those humans outside the organizational environment who are served by the policies of the social group comprising the organization. Public organization via political participation also entails satisfaction of those concrete social needs faced by participants within the work situations of organizational environments. When it comes to self-and-group determination for both participants and others, the critically public organization is viewed as reflecting the political commitment of the larger society to democratic interaction and civic responsibility. In other words this commitment to participation is facilitated by the understanding of individuals as thoroughly social beings. Such social undertaking provides, in turn, a necessary foundation for psychopolitical development. Psychopolitical development is envisioned as a developmental orientation needed for both political development and personal growth for daily, intersubjective existence. It is, thus, a mode of development vital to humans for enhancing participation in the everyday life of organizational settings. Put simply, the social, political, and psychological development of human beings fostered by this orientation serves to reinforce participation. Furthermore, such development is viewed as essential to the institutionalization of social authority in democratic interaction.

Therefore, participation, psychopolitical development, and sociality, as pointed out in Chapter 5, interact with and mutually sustain one another at the level of everyday situations encountered in the organization. In this interaction, they make democracy both a personal and a collective "way of life" in the most concrete area of human involvement, the daily work environment.

By securing a commitment to democracy at this most basic realm of human existence, practical prospects are therefore provided for an institutional commitment, over time, to democracy as a "way of life" in the larger culture. Moreover, this commitment is necessary for the health of the body politic. Fundamental to the critical view of a more authentic public organizational model is the assumption that, in order for the greater society to possess political health (i.e., health as equated with democracy), its member public organizations must also possess political health.

There are several tasks essential to this reconstruction enterprise. First, for example, the grounding of democratic values, as opposed to the concern with efficiency and the traditions of "Scientific Management" and corporate business management, is raised in Chapter 1. Second, the need for a form of reason and a language suitable for articulating human needs expressed in daily social reality is viewed as basic in resolving the rationality issue taken up in Chapter 2. Third, the problem addressed in Chapter 3 concerns the need for recognition and actualization of sociality as contrasted with methodological individualism. Chapter 4, the last analytic chapter of other theorists, demonstrates that the role of comprehensive human development is a legitimate and crucial concern. It also shows that self-development is an inadequate mode of growth for authentic public organization.

Chapter 5 exhibits how the critical model emphasizes the need to integrate comprehensive human development concerns with the equally vital need for situated democracy, that is, collaborative involvement by those persons in or served by organizations. The notion of situated democracy entails both self and collective determination in the everyday work situations of organizational existence.

Finally, in the Appendix the more critically public model of organization is viewed along the lines of different organizational dimensions. Also, the critical model is compared and contrasted with the formal bureaucratic management model.

NOTES

1. Alan Wolfe, *The Limits of Legitimacy* (New York: The Free Press, 1977), p. ix.

2. In addition to Wolfe's lucid study of political power in the modern state, the structural foundations of contemporary state power and organizations have been critically analyzed by R. Jeffrey Lustig, *Corporate Liberalism: The Origins of Modern American Political Theory, 1890-1920* (Berkeley: University of California Press, 1982); see also the parallel work of Stephen Skowronek, *Building a New American State: The Expansion of National Administrative Capacities, 1877-1920* (Cambridge: Cambridge University Press, 1982).

3. Max Weber, in Ursula Jaerisch, "Max Weber's Contribution to the Sociology of Culture," in *Max Weber and Sociology Today*, ed. Ottom Stamper (New York: Harper Torchbooks, 1971), pp. 224-226. Also see Karl Loewith, "Weber's Interpretation of the Bourgeois-Capitalistic World in Terms of the Guiding Principle of 'Rationalization,'" in *Max Weber*, ed. Dennis Wrong (Englewood Cliffs, N.J.: Prentice Hall, 1970), pp. 108-117; also useful is Wolfgang Mommsen, "Rationalization and Myth in Weber's Thought," in *The Political and Social Theory of Max Weber* (Chicago: University of Chicago Press, 1989), pp. 133-144.

4. This includes "all that contributes to the good life," as T. A. Sinclair observes in his "Translator's Introduction"; see Aristotle, *The Politics*, rev. ed. trans. T. A. Sinclair and revised and represented by Trevor Saunders (New York: Penguin 1981), p. 40, and Aristotle's discussion on pp. 54-61.

5. Peter Riesenberg, *Citizenship in the Western Tradition: Plato to Rousseau* (Chapel Hill: University of North Carolina Press, 1992), p. 24.

6. Sheldon S. Wolin, *Politics and Vision: Continuity and Innovation in Western Political Thought* (Boston: Little, Brown and Company, 1960), pp. 57-58.

7. Aristotle, *The Politics*, p. 61.

8. Ibid.

9. Wolin, *Politics and Vision*, p. 9.

10. The use of the Greek term *koinos* by Thucydides et al., in *Theological Dictionary of the New Testament*, ed. Gerard Kittle, (Grand Rapids, Mich.: William B. Eerdmans, 1965), Vol. 3, p. 790.

11. Wolin, *Politics and Vision*, p. 42.

12. Ibid.

13. Jurgen Habermas, "The Public Sphere," *New German Critique* 1, 3 (Fall, 1974), p. 50; also see Craig Calhoun, "Habermas and the Public Sphere," in *Habermas and the Public Sphere* ed. Craig Calhoun (Cambridge, Mass.: MIT Press, 1993), pp. 1-14; also, for an extended analysis, see Jurgen Habermas, *The Structural Transformation of the Public Sphere: An Inquiry into a Category of Bourgeois Society* (Cambridge, Mass.: MIT. Press, 1989).

14. Peter Hohendal, "Jurgen Habermas: The Public Sphere," *New German Critique* 1, 3 (Fall, 1974), p. 46.

15. Habermas, "The Public Sphere," p. 49.

16. Robert B. Denhardt, *Theories of Public Organization* (Monterey, Calif.: Brooks/Cole Publishing Company, 1984), p. 40.

17. John Dewey, *The Public and Its Problems* (Athens, Ohio Swallow Press, 1927), pp. 147-208.

18. Ibid., pp. 123-137.

1

Gulick's Administrative Organization

Among the most prominent of all theories of organization in American public administration over the past sixty years is that of Luther Gulick. This chapter considers his perspective, formulated during the Great Depression, as a model for public organization. The specific focus is the apparent absence of concern for the "public" dimension in Gulick's writings on organization. This absence of concern is manifested in the neglect of the realm of the public in Gulick's monocentric or one-center-of-authority model of organization. By "public" neglect is meant the absence of explicit emphasis upon democratic values, support for common involvement, and a concern for human development among members of the organization. Clarification of this issue entails accounting analytically for Gulick's emphasis on efficiency. It also involves drawing out the subsequent implications of the paramount importance accorded to efficiency as a value for humans working in organizations structured on his theory. This includes elucidating the meanings this efficiency has for humans in terms of who is best served by such a value priority and how it is served.

Since the early decades of this century, Gulick's works have significantly influenced not only organization but the theory and practice of government administration. By the time of his death in the early 1990s (at more than one hundred years of age) Gulick was universally regarded as one of American public administration's most important contributors. Indeed, he distinguished himself over this period of time

as a university teacher, a prolific scholar, a consultant, and a prac-
ticing administrator. For example, Gulick served as one of the first
presidents of the American Society for Public Administration; president, chair, and chair emeritus of the Institute of Public Administration in an association that spanned more than seventy years; Eaton
Professor of Municipal Science and Administration at Columbia University; city administrator of New York: and one of two principal
members of President Franklin D. Roosevelt's New Deal braintrust
serving on the Committee on Administrative Management.[1] There are
very few, if any, individuals who have had a more profound impact
on modern public administration than Luther Gulick.

Gulick established his prominence as a scholar in New York by
the late Progressive era, and it was during these prewar years of the
1930s that his reputation emerged nationally. During FDR's early administrations, Gulick became a leading proponent for reorganizing the
national government. Specifically, he was a central figure in advanc-
ing the unprecedented role to be played by administrative management in government operations of later generations. His influence in
this era included facilitating the role of administration in government,
designing how such administration could be organized, and articulating for what and for whose purposes this administrative role could
serve. By the mid-thirties, Gulick's commitment to administration had
focused on the functional organization itself. This can be readily seen
in his now classic essay "Notes on the Theory of Organization."[2]
Gulick's views on organization have been instrumental to the supremacy, if not literally the dominance, that the administrative management perspective has assumed in governmental bureaucracies over the
past sixty-five years.

A PRIORITY IN EFFICIENT OPERATIONS

In Gulick's orientation, the basic purpose of organization from the
administrative management perspective is efficiency. Moreover, his
model designs "efficiency" into the organizational structure. Indeed,
the functions and processes of his organizational theory insure that
"efficient operations" will be the fundamental criterion of organization
or synonymous for administrative management. Thus efficient operations become an inevitability in organization instead of simply being

"the" value[3] that Gulick insists all administrators should strive to choose. The adoption of his model actually builds in efficient operations. Thus the normative choice of values other than efficiency is eliminated. Not only are other values subordinated or even foreclosed by efficient operations, but also efficiency's predominance presents serious implications for humans employed in functional organizations premised on Gulick's theory.

GULICK AND THE MODERN
ADMINISTRATIVE STATE

Gulick's views on administration, as well as organization, during the decade of the thirties were conditioned by historically specific cultural and political influences. His theoretical orientation was reflective of the modern liberal or Progressive outlook toward the structure of political economy. In a word, Gulick's perspective on administration and organization lies within the New Nationalist or what is today called the Progressive era approach to state power. According to R. Jeffrey Lustig's analysis of the contemporary liberal state, *Corporate Liberalism: The Origins of Modern American Political Theory*, this Progressive outlook was very much an orientation dedicated to both private property and regulatory reform.[4] Specifically, Lustig suggests that the Progressive approach to state power is one in which administration takes priority over politics. Put simply, administration rather than politics was to be the principal means by which societal issues were to be confronted.[5]

Early in the Roosevelt presidency, Gulick's writings were clearly within the traditional Progressive political perspective. This is readily understandable as Gulick was born, raised, and educated during the late nineteenth and the first two decades of the twentieth century. These years represent the height of Progressive influence on America. So it was during FDR's New Deal and the prewar years that Gulick's writings illuminated his commitment and contributions to administrative thought.

The policies of Franklin Roosevelt during the Great Depression era emerged as an experimental effort to deal with the widespread effects of deprivation and economic misery then found across the United States. Thus the politics of the New Deal sought to address such conditions by using the national government as a positive force in society. In other words, the government of the United States was to become the central thrust of state power.

Some years later, Gulick, in retrospect, pointed out that the intent in using the national government was: (a) to change the rules of the game, not simply to maintain the status quo; (b) to render important services that the market could not supply nationally, locally, and by the states; (c) to ameliorate the status and enrich the opportunites of underprivileged and weak groups of the population; (d) to bring about a shift in the distribution of the GNP, so as to increase the share going to the lower third of the population, to labor and agriculture, and to southern and western parts of the continent; and (e) to undertake and to encourage developmental research, ideas and experimentation.[6] According to Gulick, the key to transforming government arrangements so as to implement these tasks required a foundation based squarely on administration.

The supremacy Gulick gave to administration is clearly shown in his article, published in 1933, entitled "Politics, Administration and the 'New Deal.'" In this essay he suggests that the New Deal was "the decision to have government become the superholding company of economic life in America."[7] The equation of the national government with a "superholding company"[8] was meant to convey the supervisory nature of government's new powers in the national economy. Quite simply, this supervisory nature was, in effect, a call for the controls of the powers of the state to be placed in the national government as the central structure of authority in society.

The need for restructuring the relationship between governmental levels of functions, as well as government's relationship to the economic-business sectors of the nation, rested upon Gulick's belief concerning the unsatisfactory results of then existing authority arrangements. In particular, those arrangements instituted prior to FDR's first administrations were seen as unable "to respond to rage and suffering." Furthermore, Gulick argued, these arrangements were not able to meet "our necessities and our social and economic world."[9]

Therefore, Gulick's views on government under the New Deal represented two fundamental positions. First, the New Deal was to be the national government's policy expression to relieve the mass deprevations brought about by the Great Depression. Second, and of equal if not greater importance, it was a political initiative to preserve the socioeconomic structure of capitalism by using the national government as the supervisor of the economy's success. In short, the concentration of the power of the state in the national government was intended to ameliorate abuses of the economic structure by making government a partner and guarantor of capitalism's survival.

Since administration was to be the means of insuring this goal, the entire governmental system was to be grounded in administrative management. Hence, under Roosevelt's administration and his New Deal policies, the modern liberal corporate order effectively concentrated the power of the state in the national government. In Gulick's view, this concentration was intended, in part, to rid abuses in the economic system by making government a partner and guarantor ("supervisor") of capitalism's success.

Not only was the national government to be joined with business to manage the nation's well-being, but also such endeavors were possible only through the use of administrative management. Indeed, the cornerstone of the New Deal, Gulick insisted, "rested with administration." He stressed that administration was not merely to be used to "adjust government" and its agencies "to the industrial . . . era." Rather, government was to be developed into an administrative "master plan" that would give "central consistency" (i.e., "control") to all objectives, programs, and procedures of government.[10]

The importance attached to administration was deemed necessary to Gulick as the national government was analyzed as "in many respects three generations behind the business sector." Government particularly lacked the division of labor and specialization. Therefore, he said, to catch up with the "industrial revolution" the national government was to undergo the implementation of a more thorough division of labor. This would serve as a mechanism of control for the "proper use of the politician, the administrator and the technician."[11]

MANAGEMENT AND ADMINISTRATION

The emphasis Gulick placed on administration as a foundation of New Deal politics, as well as the modern liberal political economy, emerged from historically specific cultural and ideological influences on his thinking in the 1930s.

Individually, such influences growing out of the Depression years included the primacy of business management, "Scientific Management," and bureaucratic rationality.

The pervasive influence of managerialism as a key cultural and ideological component to a theory of administration rests with the acceptance of business values over political values as the basis of organization. David Hart and William Scott point out that

> management which is the heart and soul of business administration . . . means control and all techniques of human control are derived from specific values which shape and legitimate them. When the methods of business management are imported into other disciplines, those necessary values go with them.[12]

Hart and Scott note that in the years following the Civil War the primary instrument of change in the value system of the United States was American business. They illuminate how business capitalized on the possibilities of the individual and technological revolution. Nonetheless, the most significant invention during this time was "not mechanical but organizational: the modern corporation, a distinctively new form of economic organization." However, along with these new techniques of management came the values on which these techniques were based.[13] Furthermore, according to Hart and Scott, the values upon which the philosophy of management are historically based are incongruent with America's political regime values.

The influence of management on public administration, as previously noted, was given its impetus by Progressive era movements for economy and efficiency originating in the late nineteenth century.

With the publication of the first textbooks of public administration in the 1920s, administration was assumed to be founded on management as opposed to law. This is readily apparent in Leonard White's definition: "Public Administration is the management of men and materials in the accomplishment of the purposes of the state."[14] White's view here, Dwight Waldo points out, was a general outlook or ideology that had already been in formation for several decades before its articulation in the literature of public administration.

This pervasiveness of business management ideology in government, according to Robert Reich, was due to the fact that "interaction of business engendered a kind of bureaucratic emulation." In other words, when "mobilizing business for war and coordinating business to avoid excess capacity," organizations of government "inevitably came to draw upon business organizations as a model of effective administration."[15]

Simultaneously bearing upon the impact of business management on public administration in the 1930s was the influence of "Scientific Management." This movement, also known originally as "Taylorism," found its initial expression in the writings of Frederick Winslow Taylor. Later revisions of this movement appeared in the form of industrial relations and human engineering.

Taylorism was a technique that systematized and standardized the process of production in order to concentrate control of the work force in the hands of management. David Noble points out that "it was not only a movement to standardize work, but it also permitted standardization of human beings themselves."[16] Both the organization and its human composition came to be conceived of in mechanical terms. In its later or revisionist movements, like personnel management, the social engineering of earlier Taylorism expanded to human engineering. It took the form of a movement to control the human element of production at both the individual and group level through the study and manipulation of human behavior.[17]

The view of human nature presented by "Scientific Management" is a mechanistic conception because work itself is seen as an extension of the machine. Moreover, "'Scientific Management' recommends to managers a view of workers as machines to be tuned for their peak efficiency."[18] In both the original Tayloristic and revisionist perspectives, workers are reduced to "parts" of the machine organization who, in management's division of labor, are confined to carrying out directives or orders of management.

Yet another cultural and ideological influence on Gulick and public administration in the 1930s was bureaucracy, in its organizational authority structure and equally, if not more so, in its undergirding rationality.

As an organizational structure, bureaucracy is based on one single center of power. Thus it is characterized as hierarchical. Bureaucracy is not merely hierarchical but also monocentric in its authority structure. In the history of organization theory, this can readily be seen in the works of Max Weber, Woodrow Wilson, and contemporary theorists of organization in government and the corporate world.

Another vital dimension of organization is its technical or formal type of rationality. This is a rationality that transforms human-social action into rational, that is, "efficient," action. It is action logically coherent with the goals of the organizational management. Therefore, in its vocational and specialist foundation, this rationality is a part of "the increasing controlability of man and things by calculation and used as a means to an end." It is a rationality that mutually reinforces the authority structure of bureaucracy.[19]

Business and "Scientific Management," as well as bureaucracy, had a strong influence on the culture and ideology surrounding the development of public administration. Moreover, these movements were instrumental influences on the politics of the New Deal in the 1930s and on Luther Gulick's orientation to administrative management and organizationl theory.

A MANAGEMENT VIEW OF ORGANIZATION

Gulick's organizational perspective indeed parallels his administrative theory of government. In a word, both orientations gave priority to administrative management. This priority is evident in both his chapters (i.e., "Notes on the Theory of Organization" and "Science, Values and Administration") in *Papers on the Science of Administration*.[20] In this text, co-edited with Lyndall Urwick, Gulick's managerial thrust emerges not only by the primacy he attaches to the notion of "efficiency" in general, but also in a very specific type of efficiency found in thoughts on the theory of organization.

EFFICIENCY IN PUBLIC ADMINISTRATION

In *The Intellectual Crisis in American Public Administration*,[21] Vincent Ostrom identified two fundamental conceptualizations of efficiency found in the literature of public administration. Subsequently, a third way efficiency can be described is as ideology or reified activity.

The first way efficiency is typically used is as perfection in hierarchy with least cost performance. In this sense efficiency is increased with the greater degree of linear organization, specialization, and professionalization operating under a unitary command. This concept characterizes Woodrow Wilson's approach to efficiency.[22]

The second way that Ostrom finds efficiency usually understood is in terms of a cost-calculus. In this second criterion, the measure of efficiency is the accomplishment of a specific objective at the least cost or a higher level of performance at a given cost. This understanding of efficiency is most readily found in the works of Herbert Simon.[23]

However, Ostrom observes that the notion of efficiency as found in Gulick's organizational perspective is a conception that mediates the concepts of Wilson and Simon. This concept is based on Gulick's notion of homogeneity. Specifically, the principle of homogeneity, as Ostrom points out, broke with Woodrow Wilson's concept of efficiency as it proposed that the means "must be instrumental to the task." Gulick further explained:

> Efficiency in administration measured in the accomplishment of work at the least cost is not necessarily attained through perfection in hierarchical organization. There may be circumstances where hierarchical organization will violate the principle of homogeneity and impair administrative efficiency.[24]

Thus the alteration of the Wilsonian concept of efficiency required Gulick to revise the structural arrangements of organization. Consequently, he abandoned the symmetry of the hierarchical pyramid for the "lattice-work of the jungle gym" while still retaining control in a single center of power.[25] Therefore, in Gulick's organizational theory, efficiency by way of a homogeneous work structure is a third type of efficiency.

REIFIED ACTIVITY: EFFICIENCY AS HOMOGENEITY

Gulick's concept of efficiency can be shown to be reified activity or ideology. The notion of efficiency as reified activity or ideology refers to "instrumental modalities of thinking and acting which mystify social relations in human consciousness."[26] Efficiency, in this sense, is confined to the functional roles humans assume in organizational life. As such, work experience possibilities are limited in these functional roles. In other words, work experience for humans consists essentially of no more than the sheer exercise of abstract calculation and manipulation of means and ends as appropriate to one's task in the organization.

How this efficiency as reified activity presents serious problems to employees of organizations can be viewed by first examining how "reified activity" is a problem. Then "efficiency" as reified activity or ideology can be more fully examined.

In the daily course of human interaction, reified activity occurs, as Georg Lukacs noted, when relations between people take on the character of a thing. This human relationship thereby acquires a "phantom objectivity" or an autonomy that is so all-embracing and so strictly rational as to conceal every trace of its fundamental nature, which is the relation between people themselves.[27]

At base, reified activity therefore refers to the treatment of the activities of humans and their interactions as impersonal objects. Michael Harmon, in a conceptualization very similar to Lukacs, has proposed that human institutions, roles, and social creations can be viewed as reified to the extent that they are perceived as having legitimacy independent of the processes people actually use in creating, sustaining, or transforming them.[28]

Reified activity consequently presents several problems to employees: it is activity that is detached from the intentionality of the actor(s). In a word, the expressed purposes of the actors are veiled or hidden by reified activity. At the same time, the reified activity (be it a role, institution or whatever) assumes a status in everyday life, *as if* such activities existed in and of themselves.[29]

Reified activity creates a number of dilemmas for humans engaging in such activity. For example, Peter Berger and Paul Blumberg have identified many implications upon humans posed by reified activity. In the first place, such activity defines action *without* the human actor and, as such, creates a dehumanizing understanding of the activity. Second, reified activity converts what is concrete in social reality into an abstraction, then in turn it concretizes the abstract. In other words, human reflection and choice are minimized insofar as the reciprocal process of understanding totality is lost. Additionally, substituted in its place is "an experience and conception of mechanical causality." What therefore occurs is that "the relationship between human beings and society is thus understood as a collision between inert facticities. While in fact man produces society, what is now conceived of and actually experienced is only a situation in which society produces man."[30]

"EFFICIENCY" AS REIFIED ACTIVITY

The practical effect of "efficiency" as reified activity is that it limits a person's work experience to only purposive-instrumental means-ends thought and action processes as applicable to one's functional role as assigned by management.

Efficiency in its reified or ideological conception both reflects and distorts everyday work environment realities for employees of organizations. In terms of its being an ideology, it reinforces such activity as the taken-for-granted reality of organizational life. Therefore, human thought toward values, needs, and ways of thinking or acting other than what is prescribed by the reified efficiency will appear as utopian.[31]

Clearly the concept of efficiency found in Luther Gulick's organizational perspective is that of reified activity. Gulick's efficiency is found in the form of "homogeneity," which is designed into the structure of social relations that directly serve management. Robert B. Denhardt[32] has described how the the administrative management vantage point underlies Gulick's organization views. In addition, Denhardt lucidly points out that in this orientation the managerial concern for efficiency is, in effect, a preoccupation with efficient administration. Specifically, Gulick's use of efficiency as synonymous with efficient administration reveals his efficiency as reified activity. Thus efficiency comes to rest in the organization -- an organizational entity that Gulick perceived as having a "life" of its own.[33]

This "efficient" social structure created by and for humans to work within, in a manner consistent with management objectives, permits efficiency to become ideology. This occurs as the social environment becomes "alienated" to everyday employees. In other words, the social environment of the organization is alienated when it is perceived as a "thing" able to stand on its own separate from the human activity that necessarily produces and sustains the social situation.

This alienation of social structure is a rupture between what humans create and what is created. Furthermore, it hinders an individual's recognition of oneself in a situation that he or she has socially created. As such, employees in Gulick's organization experience their social environment and the efficient, though reified, means (i.e., instrumental modes of thinking and acting as specified by management) as the *only* work reality.

The social structure described by Gulick in his "Notes on the Theory of Organization" is well within the type described above. That is, his is an organization controlled by management and ultimately by a single executive at "its" center. It is an organization that he perceived to have a "life" of its own. Moreover, the human components of his organization become members of specialist (or functional) units to be divided and coordinated. The purpose of such action is to enhance and achieve, in the most efficient fashion, the goals of the organization or, more precisely, those of administrative management.

EFFICIENT ORGANIZATION FOR
ADMINISTRATIVE MANAGEMENT

In the introduction of his "Notes on the Theory of Organization," Gulick states that the division of work is the "foundation of organization and is" indeed "the reason for organization." Therefore, he suggests that the "best results" among people working together are obtained "when there is a division of work" among employees. Just what these "best results" substantively represent are subsequently expressed in his explanation of why work should be divided in the first place. According to Gulick, there are two conditions why work should be divided. He expresses these in the form of two questions: (1) "is it efficient," and (2) "does the division of it work out?"[34]

Initially Gulick does not specify for whom this work division is to "work out," nor does he propose for whose benefit this division of work is to be "efficient." These two issues soon become very clear, however, following his elaboration of the concept of coordination.

Divided work, Gulick argued, needs coordination by specialization. Indeed, it becomes "mandatory" in order that the major objective of the "director" may be achieved efficiently.[35] This use of efficiency lucidly refers directly to management. It particularly refers to administrative management's use of the organization's authority structure. Efficient organization is achieved explicitly through the roles of specialists in homogeneous work units. In this sense, employees in specialized work functions become units or the purposive means to management's goals.

While the effects of efficiency on homogeneity unifies work through specialization, it simultaneously encourages a work discipline characterized by functional thinking and being. Therefore, what is efficient for the everyday employee is confined to that which fits and enhances one's particular role as assigned by management. However, this efficiency via homogeneous work units serves to encourage employees to undertake work processes limited to their job tasks within the organization.

CONCLUSION

Luther Gulick not only detailed the need, but he was among the most notable American scholars to champion the role of administrative management in the national government. Moreover, during the Great Depression era, he also formulated a functional perspective on organization which has endured and has, in whole or in part, influenced vast numbers of practitioners at the national, state, and local levels of government. Indeed, Gulick's organizational perspective was pioneering in envisioning a new organization that divided labor "on the basis of purpose, process, persons or place." Furthermore, his organizational theory addresses structural issues such as who reports to whom, how many people any one manager could supervise, and how managers could best arrange the units reporting to them.[36]

In a critically distinguishing context, Gulick's organizational perspective is deliberately designed so as to make operations inevitably efficient at the everyday level of organizational life. Consequently, it is an organization that directly serves administrative management. That is, Gulick designs his organization to facilitate and sustain the supremacy of administrative management's prerogatives in the organization. Conversely, this theory allows no policy-initiative roles or political development prospects generally for employees of the enterprise.

Furthermore, the efficiency of operations provided by his principle of homogeneity poses problems for human members within his organization. Specifically, Gulick's efficiency is a reified activity or ideology. This is so because it promotes among the work force only instrumental conduct or action necessary for a person's functional role(s) or tasks. Efficiency as ideology or reified activity therefore serves to limit human reflection and choice based in the employee's own individual or social intentions. Looked at another way, efficiency as reified activity sanctions only instrumental conduct; any other form of thinking or acting appears utopian, if conceivable at all.

It is important to note that Gulick's organizational theory did indeed break with classical or orthodox administrative thought in his modifications to arrangements by perfect hierarchy. Also, in contrast to Frederick Winslow Taylor, Gulick felt there was simply "no one way" to solve the issue of coordinating work. At the same time, his organization remains based on "principles" of coordination and control under one master applied to the subdivisions of work.[37]

With its emphasis on efficient administration, along with its absence of attention to human development, Gulick's views during the 1930s present important implications for understanding organizational existence. First, his theory facilitates an orientation on organization as a machine tool of management. By such a perspective, management comes to see humans as merely organizational things subservient to their control. Therefore, rather than whole personalities with fundamental and diverse needs, employees become entities to be fragmented into specific functional (per managerial categories) units based in specialization. At the foundation of his theory, human activity has importance only so far as it facilitates the operation of organization as a mechanistic-economic apparatus.

A major issue arises, however, when human activity is confined to labor units of an organization (reduced to a mechanical apparatus) simply geared to efficiency, because this confinement encourages only a one-dimensional, materialist understanding of human nature. Human labor by organizational employees in this materialist conceptualization becomes merely an instrument of acquisition. In other words, the particular form that work takes in the work place has personal importance only as it relates to other objectives. Thus what is frequently lost in the efficient administrative view of man in organizations is the understanding of employees as whole beings, that is, beings with diverse individualistic and social needs.[38]

In sum, efficiency as ideology or reified activity plainly encourages a technicist orientation to man where the individual is seen as a "calculable interchange of energies" and as a "resource at the disposal of the appropriately trained." In this context, the form of rationality used by management is a narrow form of cognitive reason "subjectively disciplined to measurement and calculation with an eye to efficiency." This occurs since "efficient productivity is genuinely and deeply felt to be the end of man and society." Edward Ballard has pointed out that where this mode of efficiency prevails, people in organizations become impersonal entities, as everything is taken as an object or is to be objectively regarded.[39] Ultimately, reified activity can thus facilitate, in both thought and practice of administrative management, the view that efficiency is an end unto itself or the raison d'etre of organization.

At the everyday level of employees, therefore, this type of efficiency serves to allow only functional, linear-process modes of thought and action. Put simply, humans are limited to modalities characterized by rationally calculating the efficient accomplishments of assigned means and ends as are appropriate to their organizational roles.

Therefore, not only does Gulick's efficiency neglect human values and needs, such as personal development, social political morality, or democratic involvement, but it also compels employees into subservience to managerial control and coordination. At the same time, efficiency restricts and defines the perimeters of the personal needs of the workers. In short, human needs are defined as those that can be realized within the compartmentalized existence of specialized, functional tasks required of efficient organizational instruments.

NOTES

1. Luther Gulick, "Time and Public Administration," *Public Administration Review* 37 (1977), p. 706, editor's note.

2. Luther Gulick, "Notes on the Theory of Organization," *Papers on the Science of Administration*, ed. Luther Gulick and Lyndall Urwick (New York: Institute of Public Administration), 1937 pp. 1-46.

3. Ibid., pp. 192-193. Gulick emphasizes that "in the science of administration, the basic 'good' is efficiency." He says that the "fundamental objective of the science of administration is the accomplishment of the work at hand with the least expenditures of man power and materials." Here Gulick follows Woodrow Wilson's orthodox perspective. Gulick goes on to say that efficiency is "axiom number one in the value scale of administration" and "all other value scales should be regarded as environmental" with the exception of efficiency. How-

ever, Dwight Waldo long ago elucidated the basic flaw of considering efficiency as "the" fundamental value or good of administration. Waldo insisted that such a position was a mirage as efficiency ultimately must be regarded as a means to other goals and not as a value per se. To make his point, Waldo posed the question: "efficient for what?" So efficiency in Waldo's view must be evaluated by other values. Put another way, "things are not 'efficient' or 'inefficient.' They are efficient or inefficient for given purposes. Also, efficiency for one purpose may well be inefficient for another purpose. See Dwight Waldo, *The Administrative State* (New York: The Ronald Press, 1938), p. 282.

4. Lustig, *Corporate Liberalism*.

5. Ibid., pp. 220-221.

6. Luther Gulick, "George Maxwell Had a Dream," in *American Public Administration: Past, Present, Future*, ed. Frederick C. Mosher (Tuscaloosa, Ala.: University of Alabama Press, 1975), p. 264.

7. Luther Gulick, "Politics, Administration and the 'New Deal,'" *Annals of the American Academy of Political Science* 169 (September, 1933), p. 63.

8. Gulick, "Notes on Organization," pp. 34-35.

9. Gulick, "Politics," p. 63.

10. Ibid.

11. Ibid.

12. David K. Hart and William G. Scott, "The Philosophy of American Management," *Southern Review of Public Administration* 6, 2 (Summer, 1982), p. 240.

13. Ibid., pp. 242-243.

14. Leonard White, *Introduction to Public Administration* (New York: Harper & Brothers, 1926), p. 2, as quoted in Dwight Waldo, "Public Administration," *Journal of Politics*, 30, 2 (May, 1968), p. 449.

15. Robert B. Reich, *The Next American Frontier* (New York: Penguin, 1983), p. 49.

16. David F. Noble, *America by Design: Science, Technology and the Rise of Corporate Capitalism* (New York: Alfred A. Knopf, 1979), p. 82.

17. Ibid., pp. 264-266.

18. Robert B. Denhardt, *Theories of Public Organization*, 2nd ed. (Belmont, Calif.: Wadsworth, 1993), p. 62.

19. Ralph Hummell, *The Bureaucratic Experience* 4th ed, (New York: St. Martin's Press, 1994), pp. 34-37; also see 3rd ed., pp 2, 5-6, 10-12, et passim.

20. Gulick, "Notes on Organization," pp. 1-46; and "Science, Values and Public Administration," in *Papers on Administration*, pp. 189-195.

21. Vincent Ostrom, *The Intellectual Crisis in American Public Administration*, rev. ed. (Tuscaloosa, Ala.: University of Alabama Press, 1989).

22. Ibid., pp. 48 and 22-29.

23. Ibid., pp. 42-49.

24. Ibid., p. 37.

25. Ibid., pp. 37-41.

26. Charles R. Davis, "A Critique of the Ideology of Efficiency," *Humboldt Journal of Social Relations* 12, 2 (Spring/Summer, 1985), p. 74.

27. Georg Lukacs, *History and Class Consciousness* (Cambridge, Mass.: MIT Press, 1971), p. 83.

28. Michael Harmon, *Action Theory for Public Administration* (New York: Longman, 1981), pp. 131 and 6.

29. Davis, "Ideology of Efficiency," p. 73.

30. Peter Berger and Paul Blumberg, "Reification and the Sociological Critique of Consciousness," *History and Theory* 4, 2 (1976), pp. 206-208.

31. Davis, "Ideology of Efficency," p. 75.

32. Robert B. Denhardt, *Theories of Public Organization*, pp. 73-75.

33. Gulick, "Notes on Organization," p. 49.

34. Ibid., pp. 3-5.

35. Ibid., pp. 5-6.

36. Robert B. Denhardt, *The Pursuit of Significance: Strategies for Managerial Success in Public Organizations* (Belmont, Calif: Wadsworth, 1993), pp. 7-8.

37. Gulick, "Notes on Organization," pp. 6-10.

38. Frederic and Lou Jean Fleron, "Administrative Theory as Repressive Political Theory," *Newsletter on Comparative Studies of Communism* 6 (1972), pp. 5-7.

39. Edward Goodwin Ballard, *Man and Technology* (Pittsburgh: Duquesne University Press, 1988), pp. 203-204.

2

Simon's Rational Model of Organization

Herbert A. Simon is among the most eminent social scientists to emerge in the United States during the past sixty years. Simon earned his doctorate in political science in the 1930s at the University of Chicago. However, his research and publications have evolved over time to include organization theory, economics, computer science, psychology, and the philosophy of science. In recent decades he has received acclaim as a pioneer in the development of artificial intelligence, and one of his most important achievements has been the prestigious Nobel Prize in economics, which he was awarded in 1978.

While his works comprise a far-ranging intellectual voyage, there are specific core themes that incorporate aspects of his research experience in various fields of academia. These basic themes center around a particular type of organizational rationality and individual instrumental decision-making processes via his celebrated notions of "bounded rationality" and the criterion of "satisficing" as a mode of reasoning.

These themes provide the foundation for Simon's work on administrative rationality and behavior during the 1940s and 1950s. But analyses of these key issues are found throughout his writings and, as such, provide the impetus for his current reputation. As late as the early 1990s, as his autobiography documents, Simon characterizes his professional life as one involving a career-long search for the "Holy Grail of truth about decision-making."[1]

This chapter critically examines the phenomenon of "rationality" as variously used by Simon in his writings. A particular concern, therefore, is to analyze critically the type(s) of human action presented by his perspective. Consequently, a central thrust of this analysis focuses on evaluating the ability of Simon's model to facilitate those aspects of human action needed for establishing authentic public organization. Before the public organization issue can be addressed, however, the specific types of rationality comprising Simon's administrative theory warrant closer inspection.

RATIONALITY OF THE ORGANIZATION

The concept of rationality occupies a place of central importance in Simon's literature. His use of the term *rational* varies depending on the level of his analysis. For example, on one level he uses rationality as concerned with the organization's rationality. But on a second, central level of analysis, Simon speaks of rationality in terms of individual behavior within the organization.

In the first context, it is important to understand Simon's perspective on rationality as an equivalent expression for "efficient" organization. More than three decades ago, Simon, along with co-authors Donald Smithburg and Victor Thompson, argued that in its broadest sense "efficiency" is "often used as a virtual synonym for rationality."[2]

So organizational rationality is understood as synonymous with the economic efficiency of the administrative unit itself. However, efficiency is also a basic organizational necessity for individuals as well as management. According to Simon, the theory of administration is "concerned with how an organization should be constructed to accomplish its work efficiently."[3] In this sense, Simon's perspective strongly parallels Luther Gulick's preoccupation with efficient operations of organization. In his storied essay, "The Proverbs of Administration," Simon further argues that rationality as organizational efficiency is more than simply a guiding criterion. Instead, efficiency assumes importance as the *modus operandi* of organizational management. Put simply, "efficiency" is what is meant by "good" or "correct" administration.[4]

On the other hand, the notion of "rationality as efficiency" is not universal throughout organization. Rather, it is primarily the province of a particular group. That is, it is most "commonly used with the values and opportunity costs of activity as viewed by the managerial group in organization."[5] While this definition of rationality as efficient operations is a prevalent conceptualization, Simon's writings do not foreclose consideration of other issues. For instance, in direct opposition to Luther Gulick, Simon rejects efficiency as the normative value of organization. Instead, Simon sees efficiency in terms of results, as a phenomenon assessable as a fact.

Interestingly, in contrast to both Simon and Gulick, Dwight Waldo notes that while objective and descriptive uses of efficiency have validity, such uses are possible only within a framework of consciously held value commitments. Indeed, Waldo states that "it should also be clear that 'effects' or 'results' is a normative conception."[6] One of the enduring lessons of political theory is that practice follows theory, or actions follow values or priorities. Efficiency always serves someone or some specific goals, whether or not these higher goals are articulated or unarticulated, according to Waldo.

Over the past several years, other scholars in such diverse areas as organizational development, critical theory, public choice, and so on generally follow the thinking put forth by Waldo, Robert Dahl,[7] and others. It is not that there is too much emphasis nor a lack of emphasis placed on efficiency in organization. Rather, efficiency must share consideration with other concerns. At the same time, Robert Golembiewski, among others, sees other equally important facets, such as moral organization, as thus requiring moving beyond efficiency.[8]

AUTHORITY, BOUNDED RATIONALITY, AND
MEANS-ENDS ANALYSIS

In addition to the organizational rationality, there are other key dimensions to Simon's model. These include: (1) understanding how the structure of authority in organization influences or is influenced by decisions of individuals; (2) examining how administrative rationality qualifies as a limited or bounded rationality; and (3) investigating how administrative rationality of individuals is grounded in means-ends cognitive reasoning processes.

Individual Decisions and Organizational Authority

In the analysis of any type of political or organizational theory, traditionally central consideration is given to the role of authority within (as well as external to) the organization. Simon sees the "exercise of authority in organization" as taking place under conditions where an individual "allows his decisions to be guided by decision premises provided him by some other person."[9] Furthermore, according to his logic of organizational rationality (i.e., efficient operations), this authority is plainly that of organizational (or administrative) management.

In other words, it is not the free-will volition of individual members that directly influences their own decisions. Instead, behavior is deliberately molded by management. For example, the goal identification of an employee is a product of the individual's location within the organization because being an organizational member "alters an individual's behavior by altering the factual premises that underlie his or her choices and decisions."[10] Employees are thus expected to orient their behavior toward those goals that are organizational objectives. As Simon put it, "a decision is 'organizationally' rational if it is oriented to the organization's goals."[11] But this creates a psychological environment where members must adapt to managerial goals (irrespective of their own idiosyncratic needs or choices).[12] So Simon's rational individual is clearly an institutionalized and organized person.[13]

Limited, Bounded Rationality and Satisficing

Simon further argues that organizational members engage in rational behavior only to the extent that the consequences of action can be predicted and evaluated.[14] In *Models of Man*, he describes economic man as one who is basically grounded in global rationality. This economic man has relevant knowledge of his environment, has a well-organized and stable system of preferences, and can calculate for alternative courses of action. Global rationality simply permits economic man to optimize his preference.

By contrast, administrative or organizational man is also calculatively rational but only in a "limited" context. Simon's theory of intended and bounded rationality is the model of human behavior of those who *satisfice* because they lack the wits to *maximize*.[15] By satisficing, Simon's organized individual "looks for a course of action that is satisfactory or good enough.[16] Moreover, satisficing decisions are not restricted to individual employees but also include management.[17]

Means-Ends, Instrumental, or Calculative Rationality

Whether attention is directed to limited rationality or global rationality, both forms are fundamentally cognitive rationality processes. Both are, in short, characteristic of a purposive, instrumental, or calculative form of reasoning. This form of reasoning has been thoroughly and lucidly analyzed by Max Weber and others since the turn of the century. Later sections critically assess instrumental rationality's prospects for achieving the moral-political reason needed for authentic public enterprises. At present, the task is briefly to outline instrumental, means-ends rationality.

In the first place, means-ends forms of analyses and problem solving are purely cognitive processes where thought is assumed to precede man's social experience. That is, it is a calculative process of the personal mind whereby the individual "matches" one of several "means" to a "given end(s)" as specified by management. This means-ends thinking, as Simon reiterates, "is a key component of human problem solving skill."[18] Moreover, in *Administrative Behavior* he points out that the ends of individuals are merely instrumental to more ultimate goals. Thus rationality "has to do with the construction of means-ends chains of this kind."[19] Therefore, according to Simon, means-ends rationality is essential to administrative choice.

THE RATIONAL MODEL AS A PUBLIC ORGANIZATIONAL PERSPECTIVE

Herbert Simon's organizational approach has sometimes been designated as a generic model of organization, that is, a model with corporate or government sector applicability.

This section critically evaluates Simon's approach to organization in terms of the criteria he provides (or fails to provide) to promote public action -- action necessary for viable public organization. This includes investigating: (1) the fundamental concern of Simon's model; (2) his theory's cognitive forms of means-ends rationality; and (3) the basic authority foundation in his perspective.

By examining each of these three considerations, Simon's rational model is elucidated as serving as an obstacle, rather than as a facilitator, to everyday democratic interaction among participants. Simultaneously, his model is explicated as impeding the type of *actions* necessary to designate the workplace genuinely as a public environment.

Basic Concern of Simon's Rational Model

Earlier it was noted that Simon asserts that "efficiency is what is meant by 'good' administration." He has also stated that "efficiency must be the guiding criterion" of organization.[20] Moreover, this efficiency was previously elucidated as resting in the rationality of organizational or administrative management. In other words, this is an efficiency that is extended to each organizational member insofar as each member responds to the administrative management's stimulus.[21] Therefore, in a very crucial sense, the basic concern for efficient operations serves substantively to establish perimeters for the types of politics that will take place in the daily work environment.

While Simon's organizational perspective does not explicitly adhere to the old orthodox/neo-orthodox "politics/administration dichotomy" of Woodrow Wilson, Luther Gulick, and others, his focus and preoccupation with efficiency as a guiding criterion of organization serve practically to eliminate moral-political reasoning and consideration of other values. In short, Simon does not explicitly advocate the old politics/administration dichotomy. At the same time, his articulated theoretical priorities separate (by exclusion) political matters from administrative concerns in organization. In short, administrators as identified political actors in organization are omitted in Simon's model. As with Gulick's theory, Simon sees organization very fundamentally as almost exclusively an administrative province. While Simon is quite knowledgeable about the influences of Paul Appleby, Harold Lasswell, and others on the issue of discretion, choice, and politics in all human affairs, Simon's idea of choice is evidently a realm limited to administrative management. That is, his focus on decision choices, in the absence of other articulation, takes place outside the processes of democratic interaction and is not treated as a democratic political criterion.

What occurs, therefore, with the supremacy of rationality is the relegation of other concerns (such as democracy, justice, and equality) to secondary status. Other criteria do not and cannot compete where the priority of efficiency as rationality predominates among humans. Long ago Robert Dahl pointed out that efficiency is not a neutral criterion. Furthermore, where it assumes dominance, it no longer competes against concerns such as individual responsibility or democratic morality.[22]

Robert B. Denhardt also describes how the concept of public organization is "distinguished by involvement with ethical and political values." However, in any organizational theory, and most notably in Simon's administrative rational model, it is not possible to reconcile efficiency as the dominant concern with the "need of the citizen" (i.e., civic virtue) or common "involvement" in organizational decision making (i.e., public involvement). This is especially so in light of the influence that efficient operations have in everyday bureaucratic agencies.[23] Interestingly, in situations where efficiency prevails over other concerns, Denhardt astutely asks: "how should the study of administration evaluate German prison camps of World War II, most of which, he adds, were highly efficient?"[24]

INDIVIDUAL COGNITION IN MEANS-ENDS RATIONALITY

The use of means-ends analysis in problem solving is, according to Simon, essential to administrative choice.[25] However, the emphasis on the means-ends model of rationality conceals a more universal form of reason. We have seen how instrumental rationality operates to maximize organizational efficiency via individual satisficing. But instrumental rationality simultaneously operates to attribute a "thing" status to the organization. Also, as applied to individual members themselves, instrumental rationality (e.g., means-ends thinking processes) imputes mechanistic properties to employees as "functionaries." This mechanistic dimension is indicative of the process of reification. This issue follows Luther Gulick's theory of organization's process of homogeneity as reified activity as put forth in Chapter 1.

Simon's purposive means-ends analysis is thus a restricted view of rationality. It is limited as the scope of reason is reduced simply to cognitive calculation. It is also further limited as it is confined to determining procedures for achieving the primary organizational goal -- efficiency. At the same time, in critically assessing this mode of rationality, "issues such as whether a particular goal reflects the need, the morality, the expressed intentions, the subjective desires of various participants, or are reasonable have little consequence."[26] These situations take place as the organizational instrument is consciously designed and "managed" so "as to structure abstract, purposive rationality into the behavior of its members."[27]

Where instrumental rationality dominates, as in bureaucratic structures, the more traditional and universal understanding of reason is obfuscated, if not concealed outright. What instrumental rationality specifically conceals is the understanding of rationality "as a force not only in the individual mind but also in the objective world."[28] The focus of universal reason is not on mechanically matching behavior and purpose. Rather it centers upon the problem of human destiny and on realizing ultimate goals.[29]

Instrumental rationality does indeed provide problem solving and choice to certain "means" to given managerial-designated "ends." On the other hand, deliberative choices based in human reflection on broad policy issues are restricted for employees in Simon's perspective. In particular, means-ends rationality lacks the evaluative component inherently found in traditional reason.

The rationality of Simon's model can also be described from another vantage point. The rational human, in Simon's perspective, employs a calculative rationality in which means and ends are explicable, but not the ends themselves. This is so because, in the administrative model of organization, "ends" are a province of management. Obviously, therefore, employees have no prerogratives in the formulation of these "ends." This holds not only for policy but also for tasks, positions, or functions of the organization. Reasoning is thus reified. That is, while universal reason involves meaning in multiple dimensions, means-ends rationality reduces reason to simply a "mental process of the personal mind and it is further limited to calculating relationships between means and ends." In a word, "reflection on and consideration of various moral/political criteria are absent."[30] This creates a dilemma for individuals in everyday work life. Specifically, adopting this means-ends rationality in daily work situations contributes to the bureaucratization of work life. In becoming the everyday mode of reflection and activity, this rationality is the impetus for the process of the rationalization of existence that stems from the relationship between means and ends.

Indeed it was Max Weber who originally pointed out that what "was originally a means (to an otherwise valuable end) becomes an end-unto-itself, actions intended as means become independent rather than goal-oriented and precisely thereby lose their original 'meaning' or 'end', i.e., their goal-oriented rationality based on man and his needs."[31] It is precisely this reversal of means and ends, that "marks all modern culture . . . its institutions and enterprises are rationalized in such a way that it is these structures, originally set up by man which now encompass and determine him like an iron-cage."[32] Therefore, adhering to means-ends rationality (i.e., as the primary mode of personal analysis) encourages acceptance of what appears to be inevitable destiny, or a form of determinism. Consequently, the only meaningful action for employees within this universal bondage is merely to engage in self-responsibility. Under rationalization (or bureaucratization), this takes place as "understanding of freedom and meaning" is restricted to what is "relevant to the inner man."[33] In other words, freedom and meaning are limited to personal cognition and subjectivity.

In sum, means-ends analysis does certainly promote self-responsibility. However, it does not permit awareness of how one's self and others are fundamentally social and political creatures. Furthermore, it does not facilitate understanding and subsequent political action for member participation in the organization. So the prospects for true public organizations are nil in the absence of processes for practical participation.

Authority in Organizations

Not only is Simon's employee "clearly an organized and institutionalized individual"[34] but also an individual who "allows his decisions to be guided by the decision premises of others."[35] On close examination, these "others" explicitly refer to management.

Sheldon Wolin has described how Simon's rational perspective "carries broader implications than merely the coordination of different operations for a prescribed end." Indeed, its objective "is to create a special environment which will induce the individual to make the best decision . . . a decision most helpful to the needs and ends of the organization."[36] Wolin vividly elucidates how the authority structure in Simon's model poses barriers to democratic or public interaction. For example, the basis of authority in Simon's theory "can rightly be called Hobbesian." In Simon's writings, "the discussion of authority centers upon the ability to command subordinates." There are no concessions made to "elicit consensus or agreement among the members." The "superior does not try to convince his underling. Rather, his purpose only is to obtain his acquiescence."[37] Plainly "there is a nononsense quality about authority" and "its presence is felt whenever a subordinate accepts the decision of a superior" while simultaneously suspending his own critical faculties. Simon's no-sentimentalizing approach, Wolin points out, is without the need to create a sense of participation and belonging.[38]

THE RATIONAL MODEL AND REIFIED EFFICIENCY

Herbert Simon's model of organization has been described as "rational" in the sense that it operates to maximize "efficiency." Nonetheless, Robert B. Denhardt[39] says that Simon's use of "efficient," that is, "rational," does not mean that organization serves moral purposes or political ends. Instead, the use of "efficiency" by Simon as applicable to the organization more closely follows Luther Gulick's concept of efficiency, which was shown in the previous chapter to be a reified activity. Therefore, "organizational efficiency" in Simon's similarly reified context poses obstacles to human growth, democratic participation, and public action for organizational members in everyday work situations.

In a brief review of efficiency as ideology, two fundamental problems are posed by this reified activity. In the first place, it acts as a barrier to the political, social, and psychological development of humans in the workplace. Second, it acts as an interpersonal obstacle between people in daily organizational existence. Specifically, it serves as an obstacle in inhibiting democratic interaction and dialogue among the work force. In this context, reified efficiency effectively neutralizes prospects for more genuine "public" organizational existence. Since this type of activity constricts the range of choice among human participants, public organization is consequently blocked.[40] As such, efficiency as reified activity places a limitation on human action by which both shared and individual problems can be responded to or alleviated in the work environment.

Thus Simon's "efficiency" as ideology (or reified activity) follows the concept of efficiency found in Gulick's theory of organization: efficiency at the level of organization refers to instrumental modalities that mystify social relations in human consciousness. It is activity, specifically, that is confined to the functional roles of humans in organization because it "limits work to the sheer exercise of abstract calculation and manipulation of means and ends appropriate to one's task in the organizational environment."[41]

Moreover, it has been pointed out that reified activity can be understood as the autonomization of a social activity, for instance, "efficiency" and subsequently treating people merely as impersonal objects. In a word, reified activity is activity detached from the intentionality of actors. So reified activities appear "as if such activities existed in and of themselves."[42] In effect, this concept of efficiency reflects, but simultaneously distorts, the everyday work environment. It also directly serves as an ideology because it automatizes calculative conduct as the only prescribed manner of thought and action. Furthermore, and at the same time, it reinforces these modes as the taken-for-granted reality of organizational life. Thus consciousness toward other values or other modes of thinking and acting will appear utopian. As such, this results in reified efficiency's deceptive appearance as inevitability.

The work environment that results from this type of efficient activity creates a social structure whereby employees are induced to make decisions that are most helpful to the needs and goals of organizational management. Subsequently this creates alienation to members of the organization. Moreover, an alienated environment poses a serious problem to employees as it facilitates existential circumstances where both the organizational world and the self are perceived as atomistically closed and mutually exclusive.[43]

POLITICS OF THE RATIONAL VS. PUBLIC
ORGANIZATION

In a very important sense, Simon's model can also be critically evaluated in terms of the politics his perspective provides for everyday work situations. An effort to comprehend the nature of politics in Simon's model first entails understanding that organizational problems are considered an exclusive province of management. Second, it requires coming to terms with administrative theory as a covert political theory (i.e., politics in terms of allocating/distributing resources and values in Easton's context or Lasswell's: "who gets what, where, how, etc.").

Indeed, the whole notion of organization in Simon's works is understood as an artifically contrived entity. His thinking parallels that of Victor Thompson in envisioning organization as a "thing" or a technical instrument. For instance, following the work of Weber, Thompson points out that an organization is a "machinelike instrument or tool of external power." Thus it is an artifically contrived system of "rules and regulations" that "does not describe behavior, it prescribes it." Moreover, the purpose of this design instrument is to control member "units" designated as "functionaries."[44]

The origins of this view of organization are rooted in the political philosophy of the eighteenth-century French writer Saint-Simon. Saint-Simon said that organization was a new basis of power which permitted the exploitation of nature. He saw organization as a power over things through: (1) the rational arrangement of "functioning" parts; (2) the subordination of some tasks to others; and (3) the "direction of work by those who possess the relevant knowledge."[45]

Herbert Simon's works follow Saint-Simon in that human employees are basically perceived as abstract resources of the organization. Indeed, perspectives that follow such techniques in contemporary society are said to be characteristic of positivism. And Simon's organizational artifice rests squarely in positivism. For example, man is considered as an abstract category and is thus reified in two ways. First, "man is an abstract thing as an object of science to discover laws of human behavior" as in the "case of organization and administration." Second, man is a particular thing "as the object of that science applied to actual everyday situations."[46]

Therefore, Simon's administratively rational view fosters not only

the reification of employees in daily work existence but also compart-
mentalizes and fragments individuals into units of the organization.
As such, employees are provided a correct perimeter of choices (i.e.,
choices established by management). The rational model is very much
a covert political theory. It is a model where only material needs of
participants are legitimated since human labor is seen only as a means
of human existence (i.e., a person's labor is nothing more than a
means to material culture). It is, consequently, a theory that serves the
politics of administration. In short, it serves the existing power structure of organization -- management.

This phenomenon occurs as preoccupation with instrumental modalities in making organizations "efficient" directs an individual's consciousness to the means of accomplishing managerial ends. So these
technical means (i.e., roles, tasks, or functions) become ends unto
themselves for employees.[47] Moreover, perception of employees' own
intentions is deflected and, as a secondary benefit to management, reinforces managerial control over employees. Additionally, concentration on management goals inhibits deliberation on the part of individuals as to how and by whom such goals are determined and whom
they will ultimately benefit. Therefore, employees have limited choices because, in reified organization, the prospects for individual choice
are transformed into prospects for regulation. In a very real sense,
"choice" in the rational perspective results in compliance or simple
obedience to superior authorities.

In this light, Simon's administrative rational theory of organization is clearly a political theory but equally it is *not* a democratic,
public organizational theory because what is advanced as a neutral
and objective approach conceals strong managerial preferences.

RECENT WORK IN PUBLIC
ADMINISTRATION/PUBLIC MANAGEMENT

Where Simon's theory gives heavy attention to the internal, managerial considerations of organization, other scholars recently have increasingly recognized that there are other equally legitimate concerns
in public administration or public management. Much of the recent
literature focuses on the external interaction dimensions of government organization from perspectives informed by public management

and public policy. Among the recent work of this type are the writings of Bozeman[48], Rainey[49], Denhardt[50], Svara[51] and others. Also of notable influence, over the past twenty to twenty-five years, are many writers on organizational theory who have distinguished themselves for explicitly advocating that government organizations be made more democratic and more public. Also, new perspectives in particular have arisen in the areas of phenomenology, public choice, organizational humanism/organizational development, and so on.

Many of the more recent public management publications follow in the tradition of Paul Appleby and others who recognize how government administrators are political actors par excellence in the organization and in the political system. Traditionally, in the scholarship of public administration, bureaucracies and bureaucrats are quite frequently designated as public in the analysis of the external segments of the populations served by the organization and in interaction with other political institutions such as Congress and the executive branch. On the other hand, some designate the internal aspects of bureaucracies as "public." Yet government bureaucracies are dubiously "public" in any meaningful way for employees of these organizations.

Everyday members of government bureaucracies continue to be viewed by government management in the same way that employees of corporate or nongovernmental organizations are perceived. Specifically, they are typically labeled and treated as *employees* (not citizens of the nation nor, more importantly, as citizens of the enterprise) who must remain ultimately subject to authority vested in undemocratic, anti-public hierarchical management.

Management legitimation, therefore, for government organization or for society at large, has problematic dimensions. According to William G. Scott, managerialism is itself "in a period of moral, psychological and economic disjunction."[52] Along with David K. Hart, Scott has illuminated how the philosophy of management itself poses major obstacles to authentic public organization. They point out that "management means control and techniques of human control are derived from specific values which shape and legitimate them."[53] Therein lies a monumental problem, because when techniques of management are continuously and uncritically adapted, government is taken over by the basic values upon which those management techniques rest.[54] Furthermore, management values are often incompatible with each other, and "most of them are incongruent with American regime values."[55]

Public or publicness cannot be simply limited only to one concern of the organization's external environment. Nor is it merely a concern for the internal structure of organization. Rather, it is *the* primary consideration for government organization if such entities are to be seen as authentically public enterprises. Government organization is a public organization to the extent that public (not merely government) values take priority and prevail over secondary concerns within and between organizations. Thus a public organization is not restricted to population segments served by the organization. Instead, it is public by virtue of the commonality of its composition (e.g., its common participation, common union, or common involvement of all members, both management and other employees).

Max Weber's designation of bureaucracy as a power instrument par excellence is a highly accurate description, but he did not use it as a prescription. Weber's long fascination and bewilderment with the "iron cage" was primarily aimed at the phenomenon of bureaucracy as a major dimension of the political state and as a cultural source whereby society is increasingly rationalized. Indeed, Weber did not see bureaucracy as a realm of the public, but rather as a phenomenon of the modern state.[56]

With the emergence of American Progressivism came the founding of American public administration. It was during this era that the name "public administration" literally became a substitute phrase for the application of bureaucratic arrangements in both theory and practice in government operations in the United States. In contemporary times, these structures continue to be equated with "public" organizations merely because they are attached to government.[57] In the same way that the populists understood that democracy is not confined to formal institutions, the intellectual successors to populism today point out that the concept of the public is concerned with the quality of social relations as well as in participation.[58]

Specifically in reference to authority structure, democratic political theory has long recognized that the public is not synonymous with government. For example, government organizations are first and foremost instruments of the power of the state. The government apparatuses of such states as the Third Reich, Peron's Argentina, or Stalin's Russia all qualify in this basic context of bureaucratic entities of state power. As pointed out in the Introduction, none of these types of governmental bureaucracies even remotely qualify as public in traditional democratic usage. Wolfe,[59] Lustig,[60] Skowronek,[61] and other contemporary political theorists have repeatedly demonstrated how the authority structures of American government organizations are thoroughly administrative bureaucracies. Also, these organizations have internal structures that are pervasively nonpublic and frequently just plain anti-democratic in any policymaking context for the organization's membership at large.

In order to envision prospects for more genuine public enterprise, it is critical to provide a more humane vs. a reified understanding of organization. Chester Bernard provided just such a human-grounded concept long ago in his definition of organization as "a system of consciously coordinated activities of two or more persons."[62] This view is congruent with the public component of "communication"[63] or "expression"[64] of the general, common, or simply public good. Furthermore, and of more importance, the applicability of these components extends to the internal, not just the external relations, of human organization. Likewise these components are directly compatible with Aristotle's, Cicero's, and other classic formulations of the public realm.

Public concerns, according to both John Dewey and Jurgen Habermas, involve provision for the determination of the common good through mutual, open deliberations. This obviously includes participants or members within organization, that is, everyday employees beside management itself. It includes those in the organization and is not limited to those affected by the services or products of the organization. Public action based in public authority structure is consequently grounded in lateral rather than vertical, that is, hierarchical, relations among people. It is composed of citizens or those who "collaborate openly and publicly in the common union."[65]

Traditionally, in western political thought, a citizen is a participating policymaker with other like persons. He or she works for the establishment of the shared goals and aspirations of the common good. Thus not only is public action dependent on member participation, but it is also by participation that members contribute directly to the democratization of the organization. Orion White points out that "the question of how to achieve wisdom in public action is more of creating *effective* participation than it is of finding the proper scope of *access* for people to participate. What is crucial is the dynamic of *how people relate* as they address issues of public action."[66]

Peter Bachrach and Aryeh Botwinick, in their recent work on participation entitled *Power and Empowerment*, present one of the more lucid definitions of participation found in modern political organization literature: "participation may be defined as action through which members of the political structures, organizations, and groups effectively exercise power to influence policy outcomes."[67] Carole Pateman[68], in a view very compatible with this, also describes how participation possesses an educative dimension psychologically and sociologically for public citizenship. Furthermore, Bachrach and Botwinick argue that participation "enlarges public space in organization whether corporate or public." More importantly, it "strips away the legitimacy of organizations to rule autocratically."[69] But perhaps most significant of all is that participation, as Brian Fay points out, allows citizens to determine their own collective identity.[70]

For most departments of government (excepting those few that really merit national security considerations), the democratization and the making of government organizations more truly public merit serious attention. Indeed, Robert B. Denhardt has observed that it is essential that organizational values be subject to debate and deliberation. He adds that anything less than this is not likely to endure.[71] In addition, public organizations require a priority on the values that are firmly placed in the democratic context. Admittedly, any number of possible concerns have potential applicability to organization. But to qualify as public organization, a commitment to democratization takes priority over efficiency, leadership, decentralization, or a host of other worthy issues. Certain issues, such as leadership, continue to elicit attention, and rightfully so, in public administration. And scholars such as Rainey, Denhardt, and others acknowledge leadership's importance.

The notion of "empowerment" is another visible concern that could well be used to promote political power or policy power of participants. Thus it could directly contribute to the internal publicness of the organization. Yet empowerment may also become an ideological tool to manipulate employees to adapt to management goals, depending on its practical meaning in use (this is an example of what Carole Pateman called pseudo-participation). In this latter usage, therefore, empowerment could be appropriated by management as yet another sophisticated management tool serving, in the final analysis, organizational superiors rather than allowing authentic political development of employees as policy participants. In the subfield of public administration commonly known as organizational development, this situation has occurred before. In the work of some scholars, the concept of psychosocial development, while marginally helping employees, serves in the long run as an effective management tool. It makes employees better employees per management needs in functions, roles, or specialization. It does indeed help individuals grow "on the job" psychologically and sociologically but not politically in any substantive context in organizational interaction.[72]

CONCLUSION

Herbert Simon's rational model has influenced both government and corporate bureaucracies over the years. However, his works have not in any way been concerned with or specifically contributed to a theory of public organization.

His criterion of efficiency or organizational rationality affects organization in two basic ways. First, rational decision making is ultimately concerned with that which makes for efficient operations of management goals. Second, on the level of the everyday employee, efficiency is restricted to cognitive means-ends processes of calculation used in limited or bounded rationality. In this sense, organizational members work for "satisfactory" (i.e., satisficing) solutions to problems faced in their functional work roles.

While Simon, like other administrative scholars, recognizes that there are many worthwhile, or even necessary, components to organization, the criterion of rationality or efficiency is made a priority of the organization. However, this relegates all other commitments or goals to a secondary status in both theory and practice. So Simon's efficiency as rationality as the basic "good" of organization necessarily conflicts with other criteria. Another way of expressing this is that Simon's basic "good" renders other considerations as "bad" or, at least in practice, they become less of a real concern than his priority criterion. Therefore, it is small wonder that concerns like "democracy," "common or public action," "ethics," and other criteria assume secondary importance, if they possess any real importance at all in such an organizational perspective.

An equally troublesome dimension of Simon's model is the cognitive means-ends rationality that directly fosters the rationalization of existence as originally described by Weber. Its basic flaw is that it leads to preoccupation with the self and the subsequent loss of employees' own understanding of their sociality. Likewise, Simon's perspective encourages the ideology of efficiency, which creates interpersonal obstacles along with diminished prospects for democratic interaction.

Public organizations, internally and externally, require a priority on the theory and practice of public values. Certainly there is merit in other concerns or other techniques. However, a guiding ethic of organization must reside in democratic participation of the members of such an organization. It is these members who first and most directly are affected by the policies of an enterprise. Moreover, authentic public organization requires that political education be fostered and sustained among organizational members. Such education includes, but is not limited to, dereifying organization, demystifying universal reason and ideologies, promoting democratic morality, and legitimating "political" (not merely psychosocial) dimensions of growth among the work force.

A plausible starting point is the creation of a public action arena within organizations where members can address the questions of power, membership, obligation, and character of political action in democratic situations. A public organization necessitates a program of political education to encourage the process of participation or civic virtue continuously. Indeed, political education is necessary for the mutual discussion and shared determination found in any authentic public environment based in democratic participatory citizenship. In sum, public organization must recognize a very important component pointed out by R. Jeffrey Lustig. This involves distinguishing between government and more public type of entities. Specifically, this includes recognition of how democracy is in no way simply limited to institutions of government or the bureaucratic state.[73]

NOTES

1. Herbert A. Simon, *Models of My Life* (New York: Basic Books, 1991), p. xvii.

2. Herbert A. Simon, Donald W. Smithburg, and Victor A.

Thompson, *Public Administration* (New York: Harper and Row, 1950), p. 490.

3. Herbert A. Simon, "The Proverbs of Administration," *Public Administration Review* 6 (1946), pp. 62-64.

4. Ibid, p. 64.

5. Simon, et al., *Public Administration*, p. 502.

6. Dwight Waldo, *The Administrative State*, 2nd. ed. (New York: Holmes and Meier, 1984), p. 194.

7. Robert A. Dahl, "The Science of Administration," *Public Administration Review* 7, 1 (1947), pp. 1-110.

8. Robert T. Golembiewski, *Men, Management and Morality* (New York: McGraw Hill, 1965), p. 306.

9. Herbert A. Simon, *Administrative Behavior*, 3rd. ed. (New York: The Free Press, 1976), p. xx.

10. Simon et al., *Public Administration*, p. 30.

11. Simon, *Administrative Behavior*, pp. 76-77.

12. Ibid., p. 79.

13. Ibid., p. 102.

14. Simon et al., *Public Administration*, p. 507.

15. Simon, *Administrative Behavior*, p. xxviii.

16. Ibid., p. xxiv et passim.

17. James March and Herbert A. Simon, *Organizations* (New York: John Wiley and Sons, 1958), pp. 140-141.

18. Simon, *Models of My Life*, p. 220.

19. Simon, *Administrative Behavior*, pp. 62-65.

20. Simon, "Proverbs," pp. 62-64.

21. Wolin, *Politics and Vision*, p. 411.

22. Dahl, "Science of Administration," p. 4.

23. Denhardt, *Theories of Organization* (1984), p. 74.

24. Ibid., pp. 74-76.

25. Simon, *Administrative Behavior*, p. 62.

26. Davis, "Ideology of Efficiency," p. 53.

27. Ibid., pp. 78-80.

28. Max Horkheimer, *Eclipse of Reason* (New York: Seabury Press, 1947), p. 4.

29. Ibid., pp. 4-5.

30. Charles R. Davis, "Public Organizational Existence: A Critique of Individualism in Democratic Administration." *Polity* 22 (Spring, 1990), p. 415.

31. Max Weber, quoted in Loewith, "Weber's Interpretation of the Bourgeois-Capitalist World", p. 114.

32. Ibid.

33. Ibid., pp. 119-120.

34. Simon, *Administrative Behavior*, p. 102.

35. Ibid., p. xx.

36. Wolin, *Politics and Vision*, p. 410.

37. Ibid.

38. Ibid., pp. 410-411.

39. Denhardt, *Theories of Organization*, pp. 75-79.

40. Berger and Pullberg, "Reification," p. 209.

41. Davis, "Ideology of Efficiency," p. 74.

42. Ibid., p. 75.

43. Berger and Pullberg, "Reification," pp. 202-204.

44. Victor A. Thompson, *Without Sympathy or Enthusiasm: The Problem of Administrative Compassion* (Tuscaloosa, Ala.: University of Alabama Press, 1975), pp. 13-17.

45. Wolin, *Politics and Vision*, p. 377.

46. Fleron and Fleron, "Administrative Theory," pp. 3-4.

47. Robert B. Denhardt and Kathryn Denhardt, "Public Administration and the Concept of Domination," *Administration and Society* 11, 1 (1979), p. 116.

48. Barry Bozeman, *All Organizations Are Public* (San Francisco: Jossey-Bass, 1987).

49. Hal Rainey, *Understanding and Managing Public Organizations* (San Francisco: Jossey-Bass, 1991).

50. Denhardt, *The Pursuit of Significance*.

51. James H. Svara, *Official Leadership in the City: Patterns of Conflict and Cooperation* (New York: Oxford University Press, 1990).

52. William G. Scott, *Chester Bernard and the Guardians of the Managerial State* (Lawrence: University of Kansas Press, 1992), p. 186.

53. David K. Hart and William G. Scott, "The Philosophy of American Management," *Southern Review of Public Administration*. 6, 2 (Summer, 1982), p. 240.

54. Ibid.

55. Ibid., p. 243.

56. Weber, in Loewith, "Weber's Interpretation" see also Max

Weber in William Connolly, *Legitimacy and the State* (New York: New York University Press, 1984).

57. Denhardt, *Pursuit of Signficance*, p. 15.

58. Lustig, *Corporate Liberalism*, pp. 260-263.

59. Wolfe, *The Limits of Legitimacy*.

60. Lustig, *Corporate Liberalism*.

61. Skowronek, *Building a New American State*.

62. Chester I. Bernard, *The Functions of the Executive* (Cambridge, Mass.: Harvard University Press, 1938), p. 73.

63. Habermas, "The Public Sphere."

64. Dewey, *The Public and Its Problems*.

65. Robert J. Pranger, *The Eclipse of Citizenship* (New York: Holt, Rinehart and Winston, 1968), p. 89.

66. Orion White, quoted in Gary Wamsley, Robert N. Goodsell, Phillip J. Kronenberg, John A. Rohr et al., *Refounding Public Administration* (Newbury Park, Calif.: Sage Publications, 1990), p. 210.

67. Bachrach and Botwinick, *Power and Empowerment*, p. 57.

68. Carole Pateman, *Participation and Democratic Theory* (Cambridge: Cambridge University Press, 1973), pp. 35, 46, et passim.

69. Bachrach and Botwinick, *Power and Empowerment*, p. 16.

70. Brian Fay, *Social Theory and Political Practice* (London: George Allen & Unwin, 1975), p. 54.

71. Denhardt, *Pursuit of Significance*, p. 31.

72. Charles R. Davis, "The Primacy of Self-Development in Chris Argyris' Writings," *International Journal of Public Administration* 10, 2 (1987), pp. 199-200.

73. Lustig, *Corporate Liberalism*, pp. 260-263.

3

Ostrom's Paradigm of Democratic Administration

Whether the focus of study is on political or administrative theory, there are few, if any, scholars who more lucidly illuminate the contemporary contradictions between American regime values and organizational realities than Vincent Ostrom.

Ostrom's works vividly point out how the study of public administration abounds in hierarchical administration. By way of contrast, he has put forth his theory of democratic administration, which stresses the enhancement of individual opportunites in organizational life. Indeed, in his classic *The Intellectual Crisis in American Public Administration*,[1] Ostrom exposes how everyday organizational practices, as informed by traditional public administrative theories, are incompatible with liberal-constitutional principles. He also elucidates the ways that dominant hierarchical approaches found throughout government administration serve to undermine and obstruct opportunities for individual members of an organization. This prevalent model of public administration that Ostrom critiques is founded on various hierarchical theories. He explicitly describes how this dominant model supports organizational structures grounded in one center of organizational authority. Furthermore, this "monocentric" organization reinforces managerial rather than democratic forms of human interaction. In response to this prevailing hierarchical structure, Ostrom proposes a corrective, alternative paradigm[2] that he designates as "democratic administration."[3]

This chapter critically examines Ostrom's model of democratic administration as this paradigm relates to the actions of individuals. This includes investigating Ostrom's works to assess the philosophical foundations of this hypothetical individual associated with his model. Finally, the political implications of this individualism as a philosophy of everyday life will be considered.

Specifically at issue is a critical evaluation of whether methodological individualism, if adopted by large segments of individuals in daily situations, will promote the types of social-political action required to facilitate public-based enterprises. Before this central issue can be addressed, however, key organizational features of democratic administration will be briefly explored.

DEMOCRATIC ADMINISTRATION

Vincent Ostrom's model is primarily influenced by two major intellectual traditions. One source is found in traditional, as well as contemporary, political thought associated with "polycentric," federal, or limited constitutional systems.[4] The second stream of thought originates in classical market or liberal and modern public choice theory.

The paradigm produced by Ostrom's synthesis of these two traditions is a model radically at odds with dominant theories of organization found in the literature of public administration. His model of democratic administration contrasts with traditional public administration in at least three fundamentally political dimensions: (1) his basic unit of analysis, (2) the structure of authority and its organizational distribution, and (3) the mode of decision making and its allocation among organizational participants. A brief inspection of these three dimensions as compared to key corresponding features of the traditional public administration paradigm serves to outline Ostrom's model.

Basic Unit of Analysis

Contrary to managerial-oriented perspectives that proliferate in the organizational theories associated with public administration over the past century, it is the individual who occupies a central position in

Ostrom's model. Throughout his paradigm, he devotes particular attention to considering and enhancing ways to generate prospects for individual opportunities.

Whether the issue be government in general or public administration in particular, Ostrom asserts that it is "still individuals who form the basic units that comprise political communities."[5] That is, since "actions of government derive from the interests of individuals, to be effective, actions of government must relate to the conduct of individuals."[6] This is especially apparent in his perspective with regard to the initial premises on which democratic administration as a "general system" of political organization is constructed. The starting point in building his model thus includes:

1. an egalitarian assumption that everyone is qualified to participate in the conduct of public affairs,

2. the reservation of all important decisions for consideration by all members of the community,

3. restriction of power of command to a necessary minimum, and

4. modification of the status of administrative functionaries from that of masters to that of public servants.[7]

Structure of Authority

While Ostrom's model has a basic commitment toward individuals and the enhancement of their opportunities, it also recognizes and provides for such individual opportunities to take place in organization designed to offset authoritarian proclivities typically associated with government bureaucracies. The pursuit of human aspirations occurs through the design of multiple organizational arrangements characterized by fragmentation and overlap of authority. The multiple and overlapping organizational jurisdictions serve to structure his model along the lines of federal principles as found in the Constitution with its separate institutions.[8] Ostrom's model is also diametrically opposed to most contemporary organizational theories. In short, democratic administration is most aptly "characterized by polycentricity" in authority as opposed to monocentric organizational theories.[9]

Ostrom's theory does not advocate the absolute elimination of bureaucratic types of organization: some public goods and services may require such an organizational form (e.g., large utilities). Rather, the paradigm of democratic administration recognizes that a "variety of different organizational arrangements can be used to provide different public goods and services." Moreover, "such organizations can be coordinated through various multiple-organizational arrangements including trading and contracting to mutual advantage, adjudication, as well as the power to command in limited hierarchy."[10] In elaborating the virtues of the polycentric authority structure in democratic administration, Ostrom notes that multiple-organizational arrangements provide "the necessary conditions for maintaining a stable political order which can advance human welfare under rapidly changing conditions." In contrast, he says:

> Perfection in the hierarchical ordering of a professionally trained public service accountable to a single center of power will reduce the capability of a large administrative system to respond to diverse preferences among citizens for many different goods and services and cope with environmental problems.[11]

By the same token, perfect hierarchy in organization "will not maximize efficiency as measured in least-cost in time, effort or resources."[12]

A central proposition of Ostrom's model focuses on the concern of traditional political theory for political authority. He observes:

> The exercise of political power -- a necessary power to do good -- will be usurped by those who perceive an opportunity to exploit such powers to their own advantage and to the detriment of others unless authority is divided and different authorities are so organized as to limit and control one another.[13]

Decision Making

Concentrated power in organization may also be alleviated by other means than simply multiple-organizational arrangements. The third major difference between democratic administration and traditional public administration lies in their respective orientations to organizational decision making. In contrast to policies formulated by management and/or by professional elites which can be imposed on the organization by varying degrees of bureaucratic despotism, Ostrom asserts that "the *structure of public administration cannot be organized apart from processes of political choice.*"[14] Furthermore, the notion of political choice in his theory is clearly one of constitutional choice because as he points out, "the tasks of establishing and altering organizational arrangements in a democratic society is [sic] to be conceived as a problem in constitutional decision-making."[15]

This decision-making mode, however, is not limited to structural arrangements. In a recent revision and expansion of *The Political Theory of a Compound Republic*, Ostrom argues that constitutional choice "need not" be limited to constitutional conventions or amendments pertaining to the national government. Rather, he says, such choices "can apply to all institutions of human governance." Therefore, according to Ostrom, a constitution can "be defined as a set of rules that specify the terms and conditions of government."[16] In a specific conceptualization of what is meant by constitutional choice in his model, Ostrom argues that it is "simply a choice of decision rules assigning decision-making capabilities among a community of people for making future decisions in the conduct of an organization or an enterprise."[17]

According to his view, such decision rules originate with assumptions common to a model of man found in the works of Thomas Hobbes and also in that of Alexander Hamilton and James Madison. The common assumptions of the model of man that Ostrom finds in these classical political theorists can be summarized as: (1) Individual humans are the "basic units for forming any political community." (2) Decision rules order relationships in any association, that is, decision rules are propositions that "assign decision-making capabilities in social relationships" insofar as they limit choice "as a necessary condition" for insuring predictability. As such, discretion is permitted for the pursuit of some possibilities to the exclusion of others. Consequently, "if actions injurious to others can be excluded from the domain of choice, the human welfare would be enhanced by the possibility of lawful possibility."

Furthermore, (3) Decision rules are wholly dependent upon individual persons for their formulation and alteration. In other words, Ostrom says that if persons are to act "consistently and productively in relation to one another," then the means must be present for "constraining and resolving conflicts which arise with existing decision rules." Also, means must be available for "devising new decision rules to comprehend new situations."[18] (4) These decision rules are dependent upon the assignment of "extraordinary powers to *some* persons to enforce decision rules in relation to other members of the community." Such rules are simply not self-enforcing. These extraordinary powers include the capacity to impose coercion as they must "involve the potential use of lawful capabilities to impose deprivation on others." (5) The subsequent form of political organization following these assumptions is dependent on a radical inequality in the assignment of decision-making capabilities to those who exercise the prerogatives for controlling and allocating the decision-making capabilities of others. Ostrom asserts that inequality of political conditions "must necessarily exist in any political association."[19]

Although these common assumptions ultimately condition the general political organization of democratic administration, they do not tell us how the hypothetical individuals may or do act as solitary persons. The following section reviews this ideal-type individualism and the self-interest and reasoning processes used in Ostrom's works. The foundation of democratic administration rests on this individualism. Furthermore, to understand the prospects offered by this paradigm for both authentic political action and genuine democratic involvement in public organization, it is necessary to examine Ostrom's basic unit of analysis more closely.

DEMOCRATIC ADMINISTRATION'S
INDIVIDUALISM AND INFLUENCES

The perspective toward human actors found in democratic administration is a view grounded in an ideal-type individualism. Specifically, it is a methodological individualism that makes certain assumptions about human nature and is informed by a particular view of human rationality and action. Ostrom's conceptualization of methodological individualism is based in enlightened self-interest, as well as an instrumental rationality that rests on a cost-calculus of relative advantage.

He acknowledges that his views on self-interest and economic reasoning emerge from several traditional and modern political analysts, among them James Buchanan and Gordon Tullock, Mancur Olson, Charles Lindblom, and Daniel Elazar. The classical political theorists his works most often cite are Hobbes, Madison, Hamilton, and Tocqueville. Ostrom's broader political, economic, and theoretical outlook, as well as his ideas on individualism, are in large part a synthesis of those four classical thinkers.

Tocqueville's Influences

Vincent Ostrom frequently cites the works of Alexis de Tocqueville in the formulation of his model. Tocqueville not only provides a foundation for the collective or shared nature of authority, but also offers a perspective on the proper understanding of self-interest. In Ostrom's view, Tocqueville's writings provide a mode of reasoning found also in the writings of Hamilton and Madison. He finds in the French theorist the description of a "pervasive motivating and regulating force in American politics -- the idea of rightly understood self-interest.[20] Ostrom sees this self-interest as Tocqueville's "first corollary of the principle of the sovereignty of the people." He infers from this that "each person is first sovereign in the government of his own affairs; each township is sovereign in all that concerns itself, is subject to the sovereignty of the state in matters of general concern beyond the township."[21] Ostrom also finds in Tocqueville's writings, as well as those of Madison and Hamilton, an alternative way of thinking about the "diversity of individual preferences and the diverse nature of goods and services," as opposed to those of mere "organizational structure."[22] He points out that this alternative involves economic reasoning.

Tocqueville, Madison and Hamilton were, according to Ostrom, all political economists in the sense that they used economic assumptions to "reason about the human condition and the effect that political regimes would have upon the capacity of people" to promote their "self-interest rightly understood." According to Ostrom's interpretation of Tocqueville, all human interests are "rooted in the self; but the degree of selfishness depends upon the social-space and social-time horizon" by which individuals make their choices and actions. Thus, under enlightened self-interest, a function of the political process is to "bias individual decision making toward taking into account a wider community of people and a longer time horizon."[23]

However, Ostrom's rendering of Tocqueville's thoughts on self-interest as being congruent with the emphasis placed on this concept by Hamilton and Madison misses Tocqueville's more sociality-based view of man in nineteenth-century America. Put simply, Ostrom overlooks the greater, more holistic concern that Tocqueville attaches to the concept of "civic virtue."[24] Furthermore, Tocqueville's remarks on individual and local sovereignty are more fully applicable in the classical context of public welfare and common freedom, as opposed to being limited to individualistic self-interest and economic reasoning.

In Part II, Book Two of *Democracy in America*, Tocqueville expresses concern over how unrestrained private interests and individualism work to the detriment of positively promoting the public good. He suggests, for example, that "individualism proceeds from erroneous judgment more than depraved feelings." Individualism, he argues, "at first, only saps the virtue of public life." However, in the long run, "it attacks and destroys all others, and is at length absorbed in downright selfishness."[25] It is essential, Tocqueville says, that men be drawn from their individualistic self-interest in order that the greater public welfare be attained.[26] In short, individualism impedes man's understanding of himself as primarily a social being. Tocqueville also asserts that it is necessary for humans to attend to the interests of the public, "first by necessity, afterward by choice." In other words, "what was intentional becomes instinct; and, by dint of working for one's fellow-citizens the habit and tastes of serving one's fellow citizens is at length acquired."[27]

The Contributions of Hamilton and Madison

Madison's and Hamilton's views on economic reasoning and self-interest are most evident in the papers of *The Federalist*, as interpreted in Ostrom's *The Political Theory of the Compound Republic*, especially in its first edition. Ostrom interprets Hamilton's and Madison's assumptions on individuals and human behavior as congruent with a public choice orientation to social reality. In addition, he finds in Hamilton and Madison the justification for linking humans, individually and collectively, with the structure of authority subsequently found in his democratic administration. He asserts that these eighteenth-century thinkers "use economic reasoning to analyze the problems of constitutional choice," but also that Madison and Hamilton, like Tocqueville, are political economists as well as theorists who "saw people using a cost-calculus to choose among alternative possibilities" in human existence.[28]

It was noted earlier that Ostrom's methodological, ideal-type, representative, or hypothetical individualism presupposes individuals to be "the basic unit of analysis."[29] This applies to both democratic administration and public choice theory. It was also observed that Hamilton's and Madison's "first assumptions" include the proposition that individual humans are to be considered basic units in establishing political institutions. The other assumption he finds in the writings of these two Federalists is that "individuals are self-interested and will seek to enhance their relative advantage."[30]

According to Ostrom, relative advantage or marginal utility as found in *The Federalist*'s individualistic assumptions about political experience is more consistent with his own views on enlightened self-interest than with a "narrow conception of self-interest." He simply rejects the notion of an "*unrestrained* or *unlimited* pursuit of self-interest" which leads "to a state where each individual is at war with every other individual."[31] Instead, Ostrom finds in Hamilton's works the assumption that individuals will always be confronted by circumstances that involve the scarcity of goods and services. Moreover, he observes, "both Hamilton and Madison assume that individuals will have reference to self-interest or 'self-love' in the pursuit of opportunities or interests." And "it is from this base that human energy, ambition and productivity arise." Thus sources of conflict arise which consequently necessitate the "design of political institutions" that depend "upon connecting the interests of man with the assignment of decision-making capabilities so that the intent of one is constrained by the interests of others."[32]

Ostrom notes that Madison explicitly assumes that "individuals will always be confronted by choosing from a mixed bag of imperfect goods." Madison's concern, Ostrom observes, is "clearly one of choosing the greater good rather than the lesser good despite imperfect qualities attributed to men and their political institutions."[33] However, the calculus of relative advantage is not limited to human passion and ambition only in the context of a short-term calculus. Hamilton also argues that it "permits reasoned considerations of 'policy, utility and justice' in terms of a long-term calculus."[34]

Ostrom's interpretation of the reasoning of Madison and Hamilton as grounded in individualistic assumptions of self-interested calculations presents a perspective whereby the political is secondary to a primary focus on economic and private concerns. That is, the instrumental reasoning of the private person as primarily a market-economic being takes precedence over the traditional concern for political morality and the general or public good.

Ostrom's explanation of the roles of self-interest with respect to thought about and the drafting of the Constitution is not without its challenges. Others have argued that the roots of the republican experiment are fully explained by the roles of civic virtue and the development of collective responsibility. These interests are seen as overriding the Federalist's concerns for the "guarantee of individual security."[35] William Sullivan has recently argued that the measure of the Constitution "was not the achievement of a particular moral quality of civic life."[36] A central concern of public philosophy in the eighteenth-century republican tradition, Sullivan insists, "was to avoid at all costs the possibility of despotism and its forerunner, the encouragement of exclusive self-interest. They sought to promote civic virtue through an active public life built up through an egalitarian spirit of self-restraint and mutual aid."[37] Sullivan notes further that the untrammeled pursuit of self-interest was seen by the "Real Whig" republicans as drawing men away "from their full development as ethical persons" and thereby "undermining the civic spirit on which liberty depended."[38]

Therefore, the model of man and the perspective on human action found in the writings of Hamilton and Madison contrast sharply with the views of their republican opposition. Their opponents argued for a morality wherein man is recognized as a social creature who engages in a public ethos as a political citizen. It is a perspective oriented to cultivating a civil spirit and a democratic ethics for collective participation in the determination of the common good. In contrast, the self-interest individualism of Madison and Hamilton is, at base, an economic and strategic view of human action.[39]

The Influence of Thomas Hobbes

Another significant influence on the type of individualism found in democratic administration is found in the writings of Thomas Hobbes. Hobbes' impact on Ostrom's thinking is apparent with respect to both enlightened self-interest and methodological individualism. While Ostrom rejects the Hobbesian "unitary theory of sovereignty" in favor of political theory grounded in "a general theory of limited constitutions,"[40] his individualism is clearly conditioned by Hobbes' works.

Self-interest in Ostrom's view, as noted, is dependent on a right understanding or an enlightened understanding. Enlightened understanding is necessary, he says, to avoid the "blind, unlimited pursuit of self-interest." Following his interpretation of Tocqueville, Ostrom suggests, "learning occurs and self-interest becomes enlightened." Therefore, enlightened self-interest can be a useful assumption about human behavior to the extent that the "relevant choice situation is made explicit -- i.e., the rule structure and the nature of goods is established."[41]

Furthermore, the right understanding of self-interest in Ostrom's perspective "is consistent with the moral precepts in Hobbes' law of nature." How his, Tocqueville's and Hobbes' views are seen as compatible in this context is apparent because of the interaction that occurs among individuals.

> Individuals find that instead of realizing their own preservation, as they would prefer, they are each threatened with their own extinction. Hobbes conjectures that individuals who find themselves confronting such a puzzle will then resort to reason and think through the conditions -- the moral precepts -- that will enable them to realize a state of peace rather than war. . . . Hobbes bases his analysis upon implications that follow from recognizing the essential capabilities and desires of others. He assumes individuals will be prepared to order their preferences so long as others do so too.[42]

Ostrom also identifies with Hobbes' notion of methodological individualism. This is evident in his remarks regarding "some basic understanding about human nature." Ostrom notes that "perhaps the most distinctive characteristic of human beings is their capacity for learning." In turn, learning entails the "development of an image about the order of events and relationships that occur."[43] Each individual can also "calculate the probable consequences that can be expected to flow from alternative courses of action." Moreover, these courses of action derive from instrumental forms of knowledge. This brings the issue of choice into consideration, and choice "is a process of selection that derives" from individuals weighing alternatives in terms of preferences. Ostrom insists that "in forms of voluntary action each individual will take" his own preferences into account. Thus humans can never be seen as "perfectly obedience automata" because whenever "discretion is exercised, individuals can be expected to consider their own interests in the actions they take."[44]

On the basis of these assumptions, Ostrom asks rhetorically, "how do we take account of the strategies that individuals can be expected to pursue?" According to his perspective, two strategies are available. One is to provide individuals with opportunities to interact with one another, communicating their preferences. But Ostrom sees this as merely a complimentary method to a more fundamental strategy of methodological individualism that also involves instrumental reasoning. This more basic strategy relies on "the presumption that humans share a similitude of thoughts and passions, and by taking the perspective of others, attempt to understand the basic structure and logic of their situation and infer the strategy they are likely to pursue. This is essentially the strategy inherent in methodological individualism".[45]

Ostrom's orientation here closely parallels his interpretation of Hobbes' "basic methodological stance", which he finds in Hobbes' "Kingdom of God by Nature." Of Hobbes position, Ostrom says that humans are potentially self-knowing creatures that share similar passions and thoughts characteristic of all mankind. While individual personalities have their own idiosyncracies, they share a more basic structure of thoughts and passions common to all human beings. Therefore, by reflecting upon the way one thinks and acts, a person "can come to an understanding of oneself as an *autonomous creature* and use one's reflective knowledge" to order one's life so as to enable oneself to become a responsible being, in relating to both other humans and other forms of being.[46] Thus both Ostrom's and Hobbes' views on methodological individualism are in essential harmony in that each sees man as fundamentally an autonomous or self-knowing being who seeks to comprehend and act responsibly through strategic thinking.

ORIGINS OF OSTROM'S VIEWS ON HUMAN NATURE AND POLITICAL SOCIETY

The concept of the individual found in Ostrom's paradigm can be identified in political philosophy by the value emphasis and the mode of reasoning associated with his hypothetical individual. It entails autonomous actors who embrace an enlightened understanding of self-interest and who employ calculative reasoning to determine both short- and long-term advantage. Likewise, his political society is one of constitutionalism located in polycentric organizational structures as human artifacts.

In the broad sweep of western political economy, Ostrom's approach is clearly within the natural law tradition. How democratic administration derives originally from this tradition is apparent in at least three ways. First, it is evident in Ostrom's concern for the individual as the basic unit of analysis. Second, it is prevalent in the primacy he attaches to a means-ends rationality of the ideal-type individual. Third, the types of interaction envisioned between individuals in multi-organizational arrangements is also well within the natural law orientation.

Natural law's pervasiveness in the structure of western political economy has long been acknowledged. Its influence on human consciousness in America is also widely recognized. Jon Wisman, for example, has explicated natural law's philosophical foundations, its historical evolution, and, indeed, its impact on human thought in modern political economy. Wisman notes that, by the late eighteenth century, "the sphere of the market activity had progressed to the point that it could no longer be viewed as guided or regulated by either divine or civil authority." What was required was a "secular frame of reference, within which the laws of motion of markets could be explained." Since such "laws had long been worked out," the task that remained was "to sever the dependence of these laws on the legitimation contexts of religion and central political authority." This break, he continues, "came with the maturation of a new secular cosmology built on a mechanical analogy. The universe, social as well as physical, was to be viewed as functioning mechanically according to Natural Law."[47]

While it was a mechanistic cosmology used to depict the natural order, natural law was also "readily adopted to depict the economic order." In other words, it "was transformed to refer to mechanistic market interactions of atomlike individuals. Thus, the laws of nature that regulate social interaction would

> not differ from those laws which are operative in a mechan-
> ical physical universe. Just as the force of gravity was seen as
> the motor force and cosmic glue which propelled and held the
> physical world harmoniously together so individual self-inter-
> est could be seen as providing the driving force and social
> glue force which motivated and cohered the economic order.[48]

Consequently, with the rendering of natural law by Thomas Hobbes, attempts were progressively made to legitimate political power not by traditional political morality or religious authority but by purposive-rational criteria.[49] It was through natural law that modern economic thought became a powerful source of legitimation in the contemporary state. Also, on the daily level of human interaction, it was through natural law that "instrumental or means-ends rationality stemming from purposive-rational action came increasingly to characterize human consciousness."[50]

This transformation in human consciousness did more than merely weaken traditional religious-political authority. In effect, it compelled the legitimation of state authority to arise from the "materialist realm of economic activity." As such, political authority was to be "rendered subservient to economic activity." This development, however, served to alter the understanding of the role of the state in fundamental ways. Moreover, this altered understanding is not only found in Hobbes but also in the Federalists Madison and Hamilton and down to Ostrom and other public choice theorists.[51] Specifically, this modern understanding is one in which "the role of the state was in effect reduced from that of guiding economic affairs to that of providing a suitable legal and political framework within which economic affairs might be left to themselves."[52] The state, in other words, is reduced to little more than a market apparatus.

The influence of natural law, therefore, serves as a powerful im-

petus in the formulation of Ostrom's thought. It is readily acknowledged by Ostrom, as well as by the theorists upon whom he draws,
for example, classic and modern public choice theorists such as
Buchanan and Tullock. This is evident in both his basic unit of analysis and in the structure of democratic administration. First, for instance, in opposition to hierarchical bureaucracy, Ostrom's multiple-
organizational arrangements are conceived as "fundamentally different
structures" envisioned as "providing a variety of market-type relationships in the public sector."[53] Second, it is within these polycentric organizations that collective action is seen as facilitated. Yet the concept of collective action in Ostrom's paradigm is a restrictive conceptualization of collective action. Put simply, his action, like Buchanan
and Tullock's, is merely aggregate action of atomized individuals.
That is, in their view, collective action is understood as "actions of
individuals when they choose to accomplish purposes collectively rather than individually, and government is seen as nothing more than
a set of purposes, the machine, which allows collective action to take
place."[54]

Ostrom has argued that the economic man of the natural law tradition "is replaced by 'man' the decision-maker,"[55] but his grounding
of the ideal person's singular and collective choice remains firmly
based on atomistic assumptions, market-type interactions, and the pur-
posive-rationality dimensions central to natural law cosmology. While
his individualism moderates pure self-interest with a calculus of relative advantage in choice decisions based on weighing and ranking op-
tions from "more" or "less" alteratives, Ostrom's perspective remains
rooted in the laws of nature tradition and its primacy in economics.[56]

DEMOCRATIC ADMINISTRATION'S INDIVIDUALISM
AND POLITICAL ACTION

The ideal-type individualism found in Ostrom's democratic administration is problematic in two ways. First, this individualism is unlikely to promote the type of human action needed for public enterprises. Second, it also presents obstacles to humans adopting his individualism as a way of life in that it hinders their understanding of
themselves as social beings and as active participants in reforming or
reconstructing social reality.

Ostrom's Individualism: Private or Public Action?

The foundation assumptions of democratic administration in individuals as self-interested, autonomous beings who calculate their relative advantages. This poses problems for achieving the type of political action needed to foster and sustain public organization.

In the first place, Ostrom's individualism generates the antithesis of common or shared political action. His individualism advocates activity that is primarily self-interested and is only secondarily social. It is also basically socioeconomic activity. Second, his fundamental commitment to organizational life is a private rather than a public commitment to social reality by virtue of the priority of individuals and the reasoning processes inherent in instrumental reality. That is, action generated by self-interest, enlightened or not, is a private commitment first and foremost to one's self. Thus it is primarily a competitive rather than a cooperative way to relate to others, as well as to one's social institutions.

Kirk Thompson, for example, elucidates how self-interest is thoroughly grounded in the economic realm and, as such, can only engender a politics of economic interest and subsequently economic man. Thompson observes that the citizen of Aristotle is one who "fulfills his highest potentialities in the public realm and to do so he must extricate himself from the concerns of the economic unit."[57]

Therefore, in pursuing self-interest, which in effect is to say private interest, the public, common, or general dimension of political action is diminished. In short, "the private life, not life in public, becomes the good life." Self-interest, Thompson says, generates human activity that is most appropriately characterized as political-economic behavior rather than political action. Such behavior includes "activities that are not fully public, i.e., that do not take place in public or do not involve common or public interest as a referent."[58] He also points out that "where economic interests do give rise to political activity, that activity is devoid of the concern for the common weal that is characteristic of political action."[59]

Ostrom's Individualism: Man as an Autonomous or Social Being?

The natural law orientation to individuals, as well as Ostrom's adherence to this view, are also problematic for the achievement of political action required of public organization. Not only did natural law's ascendancy help to legitimate market economics and self-interest as the "driving force and social glue" that motivated and cohered the economic order," but, just as important, if not more so, it provided the basis for the increasing legitimation of purposive-instrumental rationality over practical or traditional reason by consenual norms.[60]

So the adoption of natural law cosmology led to the development and recognition in social thought of the postulate of autonomous man. In other words, autonomous man is an individual whose being is thoroughly grounded in the subjectivity of the inner self. Socially, this view implies "essentially equal and free activities of individuals." This orientation to people as autonomous, according to Wisman, is mediated by a simultaneous view of "an impersonal and impartial mechanistic market system." Each of these views is also found in Ostrom and in his read of Hobbes, Hamilton, and Madison.[61]

By following a natural law derived from the laws of motion, economic thought was grounded on an analogy to classic mechanics that "provided a static view of reality." While men as individuals were obviously perceived as humans, their institutions were conceptualized as mechanical parts within the larger universe, which also analogized as an apparatus. But the increasing predominance of purposive-instrumental rationality inherent in market interaction and expansion provided the foundation for economic thought to become "formal and historical." Of more importance to this discussion, the basic unit of human nature in this economic thought, namely, the individual, also became "universal, that is, a-historical and a-cultural."[62]

These a-historical and universal characteristics imputed to individuals by natural law are also seen in the individuals found in Ostrom's theory and in the thought of those who influenced him. In terms of social thought, therefore, Ostrom's methodological individualism represents a specialist view of social reality. His individualism not only transcends cultural and historical differences among people, but also human freedom and subjectivity are defined only from an individualistic perspective. Rather than seeing man as a social or political animal in a sociality perspective, Ostrom's individualism is basically a cognitive process of calculation of the individual person as an autonomous or self-knowing being.

The ramifications of a human as an autonomous being as originally conceived in Hobbes were to be worked out subsequently in

Kant's "revolutionary discovery of subjectivity, revolutionary because
it conceives the human subject as the active constructor of his universe of meaning." The understanding of man as self-knowing or autonomous as found in Hobbes and Ostrom is not only an orientation
that encourages people to see "even social problems" as "solved in
terms of relationships of individuals."[63] It is also an individualism that
is ultimately subjective in the sense that mind is prior to experience.
Ostrom's and Hobbes' assumption that man is an autonomous or self-
knowing creature denies man as a social or political animal. David
Rasmussen offers a lucid critique of human experience understood as
based primarily in subjectivity. He argues that "instead of man being
conceived as a rational being who by free exercise of rational activity
creates his own meaning, he is a contingent being who achieves his
identity in relationships" to other selves and human institutions."[64] In
premising people in self-knowing, autonomous subjectivity, and re-
jecting or delegating the social dimensions of man to a secondary
consideration, the notion of identity that a person finds in the world
is reduced to the solitary effort of the individual. In this sense, the representative individual in Ostrom's model must be fundamentally
competitive rather than a cooperative being, that is, a creature who is
pitted against others and their institutions.

The concept of man as an autonomous, self-knowing being therefore facilitates a preoccupation with the self and serves to inhibit
awareness of social institutions themselves as historically manmade
phenomena open to collaborative, social efforts at reform or reconstruction.

METHODOLOGICAL INDIVIDUALISM AS A
PHILOSOPHY OF EVERYDAY LIFE

Not only does the individualism of democratic administration
pose obstacles to the social-political democratic action necessary for
shared participation in public concerns, but it also presents personal
obstacles for individuals who adopt it as a way of everyday life. As
a mode of reflection and activity in daily situations, methodological
individualism limits understanding and meaning.

Methodological individualism as found in Ostrom's model does
indeed permit a functional understanding of how individuals or groups

act based on causal modes of thinking. It cannot, however, call into question the ultimate purposes or the cultural contexts forming such actions. The reasoning process inherent in Ostrom's individualism cannot indicate why such actions are or are not reflective of the general good because his methodological individualism, like that of Max Weber, sees social action as understandable only to the extent that it is purposeful and follows a linear-causal sequence.

In other words, understanding and meaning within the logic provided by Ostrom's individualism, if adopted as a philosophy of daily life, will pose difficulty in explaining social action similar to that encountered by Weber. The type of reasoning employed in both Ostrom's and Weber's individualism explains action in a given, functional, commonsense world context. On the other hand, Ostrom's and Weber's reasoning process possesses the capability to explain means and ends but not the ends themselves. Methodological individualism involves a reasoning process that is reified where reason is limited to the personal mind and is also limited to instrumental, calculating means-ends relationships. Reflection on and consideration of various moral and/or political criteria is absent within the strategic logic of instrumental rationality.

On the level of everyday human existence, Ostrom's individualism, like Weber's, poses several problems for those persons who would adopt it as a daily way of life. First, it encourages resignation in the face of the rationalization of life. Karl Loewith, in a celebrated essay, vividly describes what occurs where methodological individualism becomes a person's everyday mode of reflection and activity. Loewith discusses specifically how even Weber himself came to recognize the ways in which purposive rationality in his ethic of responsibility and therefore in his own idea of man led culturally to the rationalization of life. In other words, Weber saw how irrationality developed from the process of rationalization which stems from the relationship between means and ends. Weber noted how what "was originally a means (to an otherwise valuable end) becomes an end-in-itself, actions intended as means become independent rather than goal-oriented and precisely thereby lose their original 'meaning' or 'end,' i.e., their goal-oriented rationality based on man and his needs."[65] Weber suggests that this reversal of means and ends "marks all modern culture . . . its institutions and enterprises are rationalized in such a way that it is these structures, originally set-up by man which now, in their turn, encompass and determine him like an iron-cage."[66]

The adoption of methodological individualism, as found in Ostrom or Weber's perspectives, as an everyday philosophy of existence, serves to expedite the resignation described by Weber. That is, such a perspective encourages acceptance of what "appears" to be inevitable destiny, That is, a form of determinism toward rationalized institutions. So, within this universal bondage, the only meaningful concept of freedom accessible to the individual is restricted to self-responsibility. This takes place as understanding of freedom and meaning in methodological individualism is limited to that which is relevant to the inner man. In short, freedom and meaning in this mode are restricted to personal cognition and subjectivity.[67]

Without an alternate understanding of man and reason, freedom parallels the Weberian perspective of choosing to specialize in some endeavor and doing the best one knows how under the circumstances of an otherwise perceived deterministic universe. Freedom, in other words, is what is possible dependent ultimately upon one's self and one's own actions in both Ostrom's and Weber's models of individualism.

In sum, Ostrom's individualism does provide for self-responsibility for humans as autonomous creatures. It does not, however, promote modes of understanding of how one's self and others are social beings. Nor does it facilitate political action for public organization. Moreover, the most harmful effect of methodological individualism, if it is assumed to be a philosophy of daily existence, is that it permits the individual to promote and rationalize his cognitive dissonance and his alienation from fellow citizens and his social institutions.

CONCLUSION

Ostrom's model is clearly a more humane approach to administration than theories preoccupied with managerial efficiency or control under monocratic authority. It is also more potentially democratic in that he starts his theory from the individual and builds from the bottom up. The fragmentation and overlap of authority in his model work also against the obvious concentration of power found in top-down organizational models.

Simultaneously, the economic reasoning and subjective morality base of methodological individualism fosters human action that is essentially private. In order for administration to be more genuinely "public," meaning more than merely a synonym for government, a theory of administration is needed which holds forth the promise of what William Dunn and Bahman Fozouni have called "administrative praxis," that is, administration that more authentically reflects the welfare of those served by organization and requires "self-generating public action which transcends forces beyond human control."[68] This type of theory necessitates a foundation in democratic morality accompanied by a social rationality and an understanding of the fundamental social nature of human beings.

Specifically, public action first requires processes for collaborative deliberation and participation. Public action necessitates the application of civic virtue in organizational life. The prospect that such processes can be developed is promoted when the ultimate value priority or the guiding social ethic of organization is founded squarely on democracy.

Second, the potential for self-generating public action arises when a priority exists for comprehensive human development in organizational life. By "comprehensive" is meant human development that includes but is not limited to psychosocial growth and includes education for personal growth as political citizens of the enterprise.

Third, the achievement of public action is dependent on facilitating an understanding of man's rationality and being as thoroughly social. Man's understanding of his inherent sociality emerges from the recognition that he arrives in the world where one's thinking is already conditioned where, as Rasmussen points out, "each individual is an expression of his institutions."[69] In short, social man is a determined being initially in organizational situations. But, more precisely, social man is a contingent being who, in association with others, works out his identity, autonomy, and freedom. These dimensions, rather than being dependent on solitary efforts of inner-based man, are socially earned through personal efforts with others and within the social and objective conditions faced in organizational situations.

In sum, the understanding that man is social, having both personal and collective needs, means that man comes to awareness that both personal and social objectives are earned through continuous and mutual effort. Sociality also provides an individual with the recognition of how his enterprises are historically manmade and how the problems faced in workplace conditions are open to shared deliberation and action for modification or reconstruction.

NOTES

1. Ostrom, *Intellectual Crisis.*

2. Ibid, pp. 13-19. Ostrom's use of "paradigm" and its use in this paper are consistent. That is, paradigm is used as an interchangeable expression for model or theory. See also Vincent Ostrom, "The Undisciplinary Discipline of Public Administration: A Response to the Stillman Critique," *Publius, the Journal of Federalism* 6, 4 (1976), pp. 304-307.

3. Ibid., pp. 78-80. Ostrom notes that Weber made a "passing reference" to "democratic administration" as a form of administration that Weber rejected.

4. Vincent Ostrom, Charles M. Tiebout, and Robert Warren, "The Organization of Government in Metropolitan Areas: A Theoretical Inquiry," *American Political Science Review* 55 (1961), pp. 831 and 840.

5. Vincent Ostrom, *The Political Theory of a Compound Republic*, 2nd. ed., rev. and enlarged (Lincoln: University of Nebraska Press, 1987), p. 41.

6. Ibid., p. 35.

7. Ostrom, *Intellectual Crisis*, p. 80.

8. Ostrom, *Compound Republic* (1987), pp. 26-27 and 201-202. In his analyses of administration and the polity in general, Ostrom has vividly illuminated the perils of unitary perspectives on authority and sovereignty upon "shared communities of understanding of what it means to live in a self-governing society" (p. 231).

9. Ostrom, *Intellectual Crisis*, p. 81.

10. Ibid., p. 111.

11. Ibid., p. 112.

12. Ibid.

13. Ibid., p. 111.

14. Ibid., p. 66.

15. Ibid., p. 111.

16. Ostrom, *Compound Republic* (1987), p. 5.

17. Ostrom, *Intellectual Crisis*, p. 66.

18. Ibid., p. 108.

19. Ibid., pp. 108-109.

20. Vincent Ostrom, *The Political Theory of a Compound Republic: A Reconstruction of the Logical Foundations of American Democracy as Presented in The Federalist* (Blacksburg, Va.: Virginia Polytechnic Institute and State University, 1971), p. 4.

21. Ibid., p. 41.

22. Robert Bish and Vincent Ostrom, *Understanding Urban Government* (Washington, D.C.: Domestic Affairs Study 20, American Enterprise Institute for Public Policy Research, 1973), p. 17.

23. Ostrom, *Compound Republic* (1971), p. 7.

24. Alexis de Tocqueville, *Democracy in America*, ed. and abridged by Richard D. Heffner (New York: Mentor Books, 1956). Tocqueville does indeed observe the pervasiveness of private interests in the United States, but he also states how he, in a "hundred instances," observed the impact of "real and great sacrifices for the public welfare" (p. 197).

25. Ibid., p. 193.

26. Ibid., p. 195.

27. Ibid., p. 197.

28. Vincent Ostrom, "Some Problems in Doing Political Theory: A Response to Golembiewski's 'Critique,'" *American Political Science Review* 71, 4 (1977), p. 1509.

29. Ibid., p. 1511. Ostrom notes that "using the individual as the basic unit of analysis does not mean that one is confined to that unit of analysis."

30. Ostrom, *Compound Republic* (1971), p. 17.

31. Ostrom, "Some Problems," p. 1513.

32. Ostrom, *Compound Republic* (1971), pp. 211-22.

33. Ibid., p. 22.

34. Ibid.

35. William M. Sullivan, *Reconstructing Public Philosophy* (Berkeley: University of California Press, 1986), p. 12.

36. Ibid., p. 12.

37. Ibid.

38. Ibid., p. 191.

39. Ibid., pp. 191-192.

40. Ostrom, *Compound Republic* (1987), p. 214.

41. Ostrom, "Some Problems," p. 1513.

42. Ibid.

43. Vincent Ostrom, "Artisanship and Artifact," *Public Administration Review* 40, 4 (1980), pp. 310-311.

44. Ibid., p. 311.

45. Ibid.

46. Vincent Ostrom, "Hobbes, Covenant, and Constitution," *Publius, the Journal of Federalism* 10, 4 (1980), p. 96.

47. Jon D. Wisman, "Legitimation, Ideology-Critique and Economics," *Social Research* 46 (Summer, 1979), p. 300.

48. Ibid., p. 302.

49. Ibid., p. 298. See also Jurgen Habermas, *Toward a Rational Society* (Boston: Beacon Press, 1970), p. 96.

50. Ibid., p. 303.

51. Ibid., p. 304.

52. Ibid., pp. 304-305.

53. John Brademas, Neil Pierce, Elliot Richardson, Vincent Ostrom, and Caspar Weinberger, "Organizational Rationality, Congressional Oversight and Decentralization: An Exchange," *Publius, the Journal of Federalism* 8 (1978), p. 117.

54. James M. Buchanan and Gordon Tullock. *The Calculus of Consent* (Ann Arbor: University of Michigan Press, 1974), p. 13.

55. Vincent Ostrom and Elinor Ostrom, "Public Choice: A Different Approach to the Study of Public Administration," *Public Administration Review* 31 (March-April, 1971), p. 205.

56. Buchanan and Tullock, *Calculus of Consent*, p. 18. See also Ostrom, "Undisciplinary Discipline," p. 306 and Bish and Ostrom, "Public Choice," in *Urban Government*, p. 17.

57. Kirk Thompson, "Constitutional Theory and Political Action," *Journal of Politics* 31 (August, 1969), p. 655.

58. Ibid., p. 660.

59. Ibid., p. 675.

60. Wisman, "Legitimation," p. 297.

61. Ibid., p. 305.

62. Ibid., p. 307.

63. David Rasmussen, "Between Autonomy and Sociality," *Cultural Hermeneutics* 1 (1973), pp. 8-9.

64. Ibid., p. 22. Also see Fay, *Social Theory*, pp. 54-55.

65. Loewith, "Weber's Interpretation" p. 114.

66. Ibid.

67. Ibid., pp. 119-122.

68. William N. Dunn and Bahman Fozouni, *Toward a Critical Administrative Theory*, Administrative and Policy Studies, No 03-026 (Beverly Hills: Sage Professional Paper, 1976), p. 62.

69. Rasmussen, "Autonomy and Sociality," pp. 20-25.

4

Self-Development in Chris Argyris' Writings

There are few social scientists over the past quarter century who have surpassed the research productivity of Chris Argyris. In both the quality and quantity of his publications, he is well established as one of this nation's leading authorities in the study of human behavior and organization.

In examining his literature as a whole, a central and recurring theme found throughout his writings is the improvement in the "quality of life"[1] in organizational systems. This concern with the quality of life involves enhancing the health of organizations and its human composition. Traditionally, the principal barometer Argyris uses to ascertain this quality of life or organizational health rests with the organizational system's ability to provide its members with personal growth, self-actualization, self-enhancement, self-responsibility, or individual development. Therefore, in examining Argyris' organizational corpus, his basic conceptual focus toward humans may be characterized by the notion of "self-development" in organization.

This chapter addresses Chris Argyris' self-development perspective as a viable mode of engendering the types of human action needed for "public" organization. First, however, how his perspective qualifies as essentially an individualistic orientation to human development is critically examined.

BEHAVIOR, DEVELOPMENT, ACTION, LEARNING, AND ORGANIZATION IN ARGYRIS' LITERATURE

The writings of Chris Argyris as an ongoing project for illuminating organizational phenomena are principally influenced by an interplay of two traditions. Those traditions represent a behavioralist application of humanistic psychology and a humanistic management approach to conceptualizing organizations as systems.

The term "behavioral" is used here to describe his perspective on human interaction in organizations. It is employed to convey the "science 'field' which focuses on understanding human behavior in ongoing organizations as systems." This includes the focus on individuals as organisms as well as their relationships to formal organization and also their interaction in informal organization. The behavioral approach used by Argyris studies human behavior in the "social organization," that is, the fusion of the individual as an organism and the formal organization, and the "total organization," that is, the informal as well as the formal dimensions of the organization.[2]

Argyris' behavioral perspective as a means for understanding organizational reality, he insists, is therefore both sociological and psychological. He feels that variables on both of these levels "interact and reinforce each other" because "the organization socializes the individual . . . and the individual modifies the organization."[3]

His perspective as a behavioral scientist, however, has evolved considerably since the mid-1970s. While the above can indeed be considered characteristic of his earlier views, Argyris has transcended concerns that are restricted merely to understanding and predictions. His more recent works are characterized by an action orientation.[4] For instance, while he feels that his behavioral action view is "congruent" with "basic features of normal science, namely, causality, public disconfirmability and elegance." In recent years, Argyris has increasingly assumed that the behavioral scientist is also an interventionist for change. In this regard, he associates himself with those social scientists that see "all descriptions of reality as normative because social reality is an artifact. When we make *is* statements about the universe, these are statements about how the universe 'expects' us to behave."[5] Besides envisoning the investigator as an observer and change-maker,[6] he sees the "essence of individual and social system activity" as "action." Action, he suggests, is behavior whose meaning is constructed by actors and is designed to achieve intended consequences. Theories of action, therefore, "are theories of design and execution of action."[7]

So Argyris' behavioral or behavioral action approach to the interrelationships between organization and humans is both sociological and psychological. His fundamental assumptions are squarely grounded in individualistic and existential, humanistic psychology.

Although the philosophical foundations and related issues resulting from his self-development orientation will be discussed in later sections, how Argyris' perspective on human development is basically restricted to the personal self can be briefly illuminated here. The essence of this orientation centers upon the attention given to the "self." While individuals are characterized variously in his works as "discrete"[8] or "meaning-creating," "action-taking"[9] organisms, these organisms -- if healthy -- are seen as "always striving" for "self-actualization."[10] Because a balanced personality, as an individual entity or system, manifests energy that has its source in various types of needs which seek "self-enhancement."[11] Other synonymous terms found in his writings include self-realization, self-responsibility, and foundation terms focused on the personal self.[12]

In addressing the needs based in personality, Argyris labels these as inner and outer needs and conscious and unconscious needs. His later writings suggest that in order to understand human behavior it is important to "understand *all* levels of needs."[13] This includes also the need for meaning. In another work of more recent years, Argyris says, "[t]he key purpose in life is to make it meaningful [for the individual actor]." Yet this need for meaning remains ultimately grounded in the subjective self. For example, he has also pointed out that the "more effective we are in making life meaningful, the greater our sense of confidence and competence, the higher our self-esteem, the lower our vulnerability under stress."[14]

Additionally, Argyris' views on the psychology of the self are rooted in existential thought. He draws on the tradition of Maslow, Rogers, Fromm, Angyal and others.[15] A psychology that centers upon and promotes a concern for the "self," "becoming," or "authenticity" is existentialist.[16] That such an orientation is present in Argyris' thought is most readily found in *Personality and Organization*. "Individuals always live in their private world." Moreover, "it is the property of personality to evaluate experience according to the self concept."[17]

This existential base to Argyris' pychological approach to man, the individual, is humanistic inasmuch as it focuses on "man for himself," "man the measure" of reality, or "existing man." In the focus upon "the centrality of man," self-development psychology is clearly a humanistic psychology. And Argyris' assumptions in the realm of psychology are clearly influenced by the humanistic tradition. A basic problem with this tradition is that (as Theodore Adorno said in another context) "the more strictly the psychological realm is conceived as an autonomous, self-enclosed play for forces, the more completely the subject is drained of his subjectivity. The objectless subject that is thrown back on himself, freezes into an object."[18]

The second tradition of thought influencing Argyris' writings on organizational phenomena is a humanistic management approach to organizations as systems. His perspective on organizational behavior, particularly as applicable to the structure of authority in organizations, can be characterized as grounded in humanistic management.

The explicitly humanistic dimension of his writings on organizations can be seen in Argyris' genuine and longstanding concern to alleviate authoritarian aspects of "formal"[19] organizations. Furthermore, his concern for more humane behavioral interactions and reasoned use of authority is also apparent in his more recent range of literature focused on learning and action systems. However, while humanistic, his views are nonetheless supportive of management.

Specifically, Argyris' work is biased toward the acceptance of management prerogative particularly as this relates to ultimate decision-making authority in organizational policy. The prerogative of management to make and implement policy for the organization is essentially unquestioned. At the same time, Argyris has not neglected the tasks of altering unhealthy organization and the authoritarian practices of management. Both his early writings, especially on Model II or double-loop learning, and even his later writings do indeed encourage evaluative capacities on the part of individual employees of the organization. While such critical capacities among organizational members could be instrumental in restructuring authority toward common involvement or a "public" foundation, Argyris' writings nonetheless stop short of seriously questioning the fundamental discretion of managment in making overall organizational policy.

Also absent in Argyris' literature is an advocacy for the value of general involvement or participation in the goal agendas of the organization. The extent to which his works advocate the notion of "participation" is best characterized as psychosocial in nature rather than psychopolitical. In his writings, the relationship between authority in organization and participation is not basically political. Participation as a dimension of Argyris' human development is not a normative concept that extends to employees as policymakers on organizational goals. His view of participation simply is not equivalent to organizational citizenship. Instead, participation in Argyris' writings occurs within the policymaking structures that already exist within the organization.

His humanistic management view of organization is present in his early writings influenced by systems theory. It is still present in his literature on organizational development, including contemporary action-interventionist writings dealing with learning systems.

One important aspect of this management orientation is the influence of systems theory. Argyris' notion of organization in early as well as more contemporary writings is seen as a system. In the 1954 publication *Organization of a Bank*, he says "organization is to be conceived as an open system." Following the definition of Ludwig Bertalanffy, Argyris suggests an open system is "one where there is an inflow and outflow and therefore movements in the system." Organizations are consequently dynamic as they are "in continual motion"[20] as "on-going systems."[21]

Much of his work for a better quality of life in organizations is directed toward seeking ways to eliminate human dependence and inhibitors of "participation," that is, "participation," as previously pointed out, within the already established structure of organizational authority. In other words, his works have striven to find ways for healthier organizations. Healthier organizations are those that can be "designed and operated so that human actualization is valued and required." By the same logic, healthier organizations are humane organizations to the extent that they permit an "increase in individuals' capacities for self-acceptance and interpersonal competence"[22], for example, through such "means" as intervention by learning strategies for more effective organizational behavior.

The thrust of Argyris' criticism toward organization has been aimed at the *formal* norms and the structure of organizational arrangements as found in the formal, classical and neoclassical, model. Argyris recognizes that this model "creates feelings of failure and frustration, short-time perspective and conflict."[23] Formal organizational norms make for a closeness rather than an openness in the quality of life and a loss of organizational vitality. Therefore, among organizational participants this leads to conformity, submissiveness, adaptation, and mistrust.[24] As such, formal organizational arrangements by a hierarchical pyramid[25] or through the use of such concepts as unity of direction or span of control[26] contribute to unhealthy personalities or immature individual development. Moreover, formal authority structure represses interpersonal relationships among employees of the organization, which, he states, leads to decreased capacity to accept new ideas and values.[27]

> The overall impact of the formal organization on the individual is to decrease his control over his immediate work area, decrease his chances to use his abilities, and increase his dependence and submissiveness; second, that to the extent to which the individual seeks to be autonomous and function as an adult he adapts by reactions ranging from withdrawal and non-interest, to aggression, or perhaps to the substitution of instrumental money awards for intrinsic rewards. The weight of deprivations and the degree of adaptation increase as we descend the hierarchy. Formal organizations, alas, are unintentionally designed to discourage the autonomous and involved worker.[28]

Although Argyris advocates organizational change in terms of altering psychosocial levels of behavior in unhealthy organizations, as previously noted, he stops short of articulating a need for a commitment to alter the authority in the policymaking prerogatives or powers of management. Also, he does not envision a value concern toward common involvement or general participation as a legitimate source of authority for democratically establishing organizational goals.

The issue of organizational policy prerogative in Argyris' writings is absent, except for his general references to the determination of substantive organizational goals as the province of management. He suggests that any organizational change "in the *status quo* involves leadership."[29] According to Argyris, "organizational change begins at the top" because "involvement for change must begin where power lies."[30] While he does acknowledge that a "way must be found to create a work-place that meets the needs of modern working man," he is simultaneously insistent that a "way must be found of attaining this goal without an adverse effect on productivity."[31]

THE PHILOSOPHICAL FOUNDATIONS OF ARGYRIS' PSYCHOLOGY OF SELF-DEVELOPMENT

Earlier I described how, in several ways, Argyris' human development perspective was congruent with the humanistic psychology of, among many others, Abraham Maslow, Carl Rogers, and Eric Fromm. This psychology was characterized as humanistic because of the centrality of emphasis placed on man as the measure of all things. Humanistic psychology not only stresses the centrality of man, or man for himself, but it likewise includes those more existential versions that exhibit visible priority for the "self," "personality," "actualization," "becoming," and "authenticity." Humanistic psychology encompasses those psychologies, of whatever particular tradition, that do not acknowledge the societal impact on the individual or see the individual "only in loose contact with society."[32] Jacoby has noted that this psychology "posits the individual as an independent unity from without."[33] The emphasis of humanistic psychology is upon subjectivity where "society is conceived as an external factor acting on the individual, but not decisively casting the individual from without or from within."[34]

In considering his works as a whole, Argyris' view of man in organization represents a moderate reform perspective within this tradition. The organic influences on his thinking, which derive from systems theory, serve to emphasize the interrelationships between the individual and the social environment. So the subjectivistic conception of the individual found in more existential psychologists is moderated in Argyris' works. Likewise, his later writings increasingly turn toward a stress on the social and interdependent dimensions of the individual. Furthermore, by his attention to the interpersonal competence of humans, Argyris has pointed out the importance of both the rational, as well as the affective, qualities of human personality.[35] On the other hand, his notion of man as an individual in organizational environments remains grounded in a subjectivistic conception of the self. That is, his conceptions self-acceptance, self-enhancement, and so forth remain rooted in humanistic psychology.

This psychological tradition presents a problematic foundation for formulating a mode of human development necessary for "public" organizations. Put simply, human development as self-development inhibits organization for genuine or authentic common involvement. Self-development psychology is based on Kantian subjectivity and liberal individualist morality.

How this humanistic self-development psychology hinders a more comprehensive model of human development conducive for a viable "public" organization can be illuminated by critically examining the ways this tradition approaches and has an impact on several key issues in human growth. These issues are social reality, human identity, roles or role behavior, autonomy, and change.

In humanistic psychology, social reality is experienced by the individual person as subjectivity. Philosophically this tradition grounds rationality and epistemology in the autonomous notion of man, whose being and reality originate internally in the self. Therefore, in this self-development perspective, social reality or the social "experience is determined by categories of the mind."[36] In this context, social reality or what is objectively "social in origin is presented as natural and human." However, in divesting social reality of its objectivity, it is thereby "psychologized away." The consequences of this orientation when assumed by human actors, Russell Jacoby points out, is that society is thereby "conceived as simply a psychological pact between men, not as a piece of reality with its own social gravity."[37] This tradition thus promotes the Cartesian subject/object dichotomy in which the world, that is, social reality, is conceived as existing "out there" or, as Jacoby states, merely as an "external factor." Finally, humanistic psychology's orientation to social reality distorts the capacity for human understanding among individuals in a very fundamental sense: "in reducing everything to the subject and denying objective truth it loses the ability to distinguish between delusions and reality. . . . Social process and conflict are read as psychological and individual ones."[38] Second, the issue of human identity among humanistic psychologists is understood as basically an individual undertaking: while social reality is an external factor influencing him or her, the individual in this tradition is not seen as a determined being in regard to identity. Rather, one may still achieve one's real self, one's authenticity. However, this effort is very much one's own. It is the individual's own achievement subject not necessarily to others, but rather to his or her confirmation. Viewed from a perspective based in humanistic psychology, the person's identity is not only one's own to work out. But, more fundamentally, it is grounded in the inner self -- the self as an internally based being.

Therefore, identity in this tradition is the self's to possess through his or her subjective capacities. Following Kant, the individual human subject sees the self as the constructor of one's own universe of meaning. As such, the individual creates or determines his or her own social reality and individual identity.[39] In contrast to this view of identity as an individual undertaking, identity from a perspective grounded in sociality is seen as a social phenomenon. In a word, identity is social, not individual, in origin.

The sociality view of identity, David Rasmussen states, recognizes that "one arrives in the world where his thinking is already conditioned." In other words, social identity creates a view of the total situation of human existence that makes the human situation intelligible. Rather than conceiving the self as distinct from institutions, a social-based perspective permits the individual to have awareness of how one is "an expression of the institutions in which he lives." Moreover, this social identity permits one the capacity to view the institutional context of existence critically.[40] Social identity is thus one vital dimension toward developing a psychology of human development for organizations facilitating common or public involvement. However, this identity is intimately tied to the notion of social freedom or autonomy earned socially.

The issue of autonomy in humanistic self-development psychology, like that of identity, follows the tradition of Kant and the liberal epistemological perspective on the nature of man. Specifically, man is seen as an autonomous creature, a free being, a private individual who is in proprietorship of one's own person. One is therefore free to work out his or her personal autonomy, as well as identity, as essentially a private affair. Consequently, the situations, institutions, and general social reality the self encounters are taken as given. They are taken as given in the sense that they are beyond being brought into fundamental question. One is to achieve autonomy and identity, adapting as necessary to given social conditions.

Thus while the issue of autonomy under self-development psychology is strictly a personal undertaking, it is recognized as a thor-

oughly social endeavor from a perspective based in sociality. Autonomy for social man is an earned freedom with others and, as such, is
possible only through others. Autonomy thus involves a continual recognition by the individual of one's organizational situation. It simultaneously entails awareness on the individual's part of how such a
reality should be different. In addition, as Rasmussen says:

> between the *ought* of the true species being that he should
> be, and the *is* of his present reality in which he is treated
> as private property . . . [is] freedom [which] is earned free-
> dom, i.e., the freedom that one has will have to be worked
> out in the world of primary human activity in relationship
> to other men. Equally, freedom is to be conceived as the
> ability to work out a true authentic identity in social situ-
> ations.[41]

Another issue within the foundation of self-development psychology which inhibits a more comprehensive development centers on the
issue of roles or role behavior. Self-based psychology uses the notion
of role or role behavior to describe thought-action orientation(s) an individual perceives and then assumes or "plays at" in various activities
or situations. These internally based roles may or may not be "in
character," measure up or be described as functional for the activity
or situation as viewed by others. When behavior exhibited is in line
with the expectations of others for a given activity or situation, this
role behavior is considered social. Furthermore, a social role as applied to the work environment is functional insofar as the individual
organizes his or her thoughts and actions so as to fulfill expectations
and/or assignments of management or others.[42] The concept of role
in humanistic self-development psychology therefore is ultimately
based on the assumption that the self is actually someone (or plural
some-ones) other than the self. That is, it assumes that the self
naturally assumes a role that is inherently not him or herself.

Russell Jacoby has shown that roles in this tradition are more accurately characterized as "estranged human behavior." Moreover, he
suggests that any theory that accepts roles as natural or human is ideological. Therefore, a mode of human development that nurtures prospects for public organization would be an orientation that incorporates
critical theory's understanding of roles. Roles in this tradition of

critical theory are recognized as true and false. Roles are "true insofar as they are not merely paperthin facade, but are entangled with the individual." On the other hand, roles are "false as they are a mode of behavior of an unfree society." Jacoby further explicates his reasoning of this issue. He argues:

> roles are not only fraudulent, they are also real. Roles are not merely adopted by the subject as a facade that can be dropped with a little willpower. They are an alienated mode of behavior custom-fit for an alienated society. The neat division between roles and real selves reduces society to a masquerade party . . . people not only assume roles, they are roles. This admission is no concession to inhumanity. Rather in articulating the full strength of the prevailing inhumanity it holds forth the hope of material transcendence. The insistence, on the other hand, of finding humanity everywhere by underestimating the objective and social foundations of inhumanity perpetuates the latter -- it humanizes inhumanity.[43]

Finally, the prospects for change originating from humanistic psychology contrast sharply with human development from the social orientation.

Whether the issues be social reality, autonomy, identity, or roles, the prospects for change in the self-development perspective encourage only personal change. Reality is based in the self, the self's efforts, and the self's interests. One works to change oneself first and then to cooperate with others only to the extent that such an endeavor is to be beneficial to one's person or self-enhancing. One works for change with others or by oneself to improve one's self-enhancement or self-acceptance in realms of economics, politics, social, or organizational status or whatever.

In contrast, change in the social perspective of human development acknowledges man's sociality. The individual's autonomy and identity are intimately connected to one's social realities. Change is recognized as a social process in which people work together continually to work out their identities and freedom. This social perspective acknowledges the individual as a contingent being. The individual enters a social or organizational situation that influences and gives identity. Yet such situations are understood as socially and historically (man)made. Thereby they are open to change via reform and reconstruction through collective effort. Additionally, change requires "social" enterprise for the individual to overcome the contingent identity, to the extent that one's initial identity is not that which could or should be as conceived by the person.

Humanistic "human development as self-development" in focusing on the subjectivity and ethics of the individual inadequately comes to grips with the objective social structure of reality and the social nature of construction and reconstruction possibilities. It consequently hinders a psychology of human development necessary for genuine public organization. Conversely, it facilitates support for managerialism by its inadequate view of the social nature of man. Man is simply mechanically "interactive" with the social environment. This is illustrated in Argyris', *Personality and Organization*, for instance, in the discussion of personality balance in "equilibrium," that is, internal equilibrium for adjustment, external equilibrium for adaptation to the person's job, and so on.[44]

PROSPECTS AND BARRIERS TO PUBLIC ORGANIZATION THEORY IN THE WORKS OF CHRIS ARGYRIS

The works of Chris Argyris have significantly contributed to a more comprehensive understanding of humans and their needs than is found in traditional administrative views on organization. Argyris' early work, particularly on personality and organization, aptly illuminated how the functional approach of traditional organizational theory was restricted to only the "psychologically less important aspects" of human behavior in organizational life. In addition, he has shown how the affective, nonrational dimensions of man are "vitally important to the individual for his development, growth and creativity." Throughout his works he has shown that such development prospects benefit both individuals and organizations.[45]

In their special regard to personal development and barriers to psychological well-being, his writings have been tremendously important in illuminating how people are "lost sight of as whole beings in formal bureaucratic organizations." Randal Ihara has observed that Argyris' early work was indeed "pioneering" in demonstrating how formal-hierarchical organizational life reduced man "to the sum of his functions (doing abilities) [which] . . . places man in the position of calling his essence, his fullness, into question to the point of denying it all reality . . . [hence] interior reality is thus reduced to a status of a thing, both to himself and to others."[46] Thus Argyris recognized how traditional approaches to organization emphasized "only those aspects of the individual which are fundamental in terms of organizational goals." As such, his writings point out vividly how fundamental strivings for increasing self-realization are frequently frustrated in organizational life. In this sense, Argyris' works provide a much more comprehensive understanding of humans. He does so by focusing on and amplifying the person as a whole being; a person with "inner needs" that "tell us what a person *is* as well as "outer needs" that tell us what a person *does*."[47]

In contrast to more explicitly "humanist" theorists of human relations or other organizational behavioralists more fully within the humanistic tradition, Argyris recognizes the interpersonal basis of personality. In this context, he sees a basic social-political building block needed for an authentically public organization. That is, he points out that "personality is essentially an interpersonal phenomenon; that it requires others to be whole." In *Understanding Organizational Behavior*, he argues that "all human beings are incomplete by themselves. They gain their wholeness through interaction with others . . . man is fundamentally an interpersonal organism. Self-Actualization . . . cannot occur in isolation. It can only occur in relationship with others."[48]

Another important consideration in human development is Argyris' (and Donald Shön's) research with double-loop or what they call Model II learning processes. Robert B. Denhardt has noted that the emphasis that Argyris places upon "learning about self and others" provides an important connection between Argyris' early works on personality and organization and his later work on change in organization. Moreover, Denhardt suggests an important distinction between Argyris' work and that of other human relation theorists.[49] Denhardt goes on to observe that much of Argyris' work, like that of so many other human relation theorists, "may be appropriated by management for more sophisticated manipulation of organizational workers." At the same time, he suggests Argyris' efforts and commitments to learning and action, which "implies a relationship involving shared meanings" and raises possibilities for creating and establishing not only conditions of trust, openness, and self-esteem but also conditions of community.[50]

On the other hand, Argyris' writings pose certain difficulties for the realization of a more authentically public organization. The dialectic of subjectivism and scientism present in his writings as a whole risks the further reification of organization experience for human participants. That is, his theoretical reliance on humanistic psychology and systems theory presents an apporach to human phenomena in organization that is at once subjectivistic and scientistic. As such, this perspective creates problems for individuals situated in everyday organizational realities.

The first implication of an approach grounded in a self-systems dialectic is that it encourages behavior that is adaptive to existing organizational rules and policies. Ultimately, in the acceptance of managerial leadership (or managerial policy initiative) and the accompanying administrative approach to organization problems (i.e., instrumental rationality processes), everyday members are still required to adapt to such prerogatives and processes. Hence such leadership and organizational structure remain an estranged reality to participants. In this situation, the organization presents an appearance of an alienated facticity or "thing" to the everyday employees. Consequently, understanding of the larger social (and dialectical) totality is lost. Lost, in short, is the understanding by individuals in organizations that it is they who collectively as humans create social structure. Also, lost is the understanding that these structures indeed influence and condition many aspects of their lives. Furthermore, these individuals lose the understanding that they socially possess the capacities to reform and reconstruct such manmade structures.

Additionally, the focus on the self's responsibility principally for the individual's own identity and autonomy inhibits cognizances in individuals of their fundamental social nature. In this sense, the subjectivistic basis found in humanistic psychology impedes a more genuine understanding among humans of everyday intersubjectivity, which is needed for development of interpersonal competence, growth, and maturity (as otherwise found in Argyris' concern for personality) and development for the social-political action needed for public enterprise.

Second, and on a more immediate level, the understanding of self and others in organization from the perspective of man who is essentially an internal-private being may actually enhance passivity and self-deprecation rather than activity and actualization. This is likely to occur to the extent that the understanding of social reality provided by subjectivistic psychology is one where personal problems experienced in work life are perceived as residing solely in one's self. Also through this inner-based understanding to social reality, the problems occurring in the work environment may similarly be attributed merely to the "personal difficulties" of other atomistic individuals. That is, in situations where the source of human dilemmas specifically rest in the social and objective conditions of the workplace, such human difficulties can be readily obfuscated in the subjectivistic orientation to reality.

In sum, the emphasis of the self-systems perspective is upon a restrained view toward human growth and development. It cannot be pointed out too strongly that it is "restrained" in that cognition and feeling are separated from political and social conditions presented by organizational realities. Therefore, while Argyris' self-development is indeed beneficial to the individual, it is a mode of development that can have equally advantageous merits to organizational management. This is especially so since it does not threaten or disrupt existing power arrangements in the organization. The very foundations of Argyris' perspective on development, where it is grounded in the subjective self, confines dimensions of competence and growth to attributes that basically enhance the individual as employee rather than as a full participating member (or citizen) of public organization. In other words, his self-development is for growth, health, and improving one's self interpersonally by criteria that ultimately must be acceptable to existing organizational leadership, their policies, and their processes of rationality values as found throughout the organization.

NOTES

1. Chris Argyris, *Personality and Organization* (New York: Harper and Row, 1957), pp. 49 and 62; *Management and Organizational Development* (New York: McGraw Hill, 1971), pp. x and 185; *On Organization of the Future*, Administrative and Policy Series No. 03-006 (Beverly Hills, Sage Professional Paper, 1973), pp. 14, 24, and 26; "Personality vs. Organization," *Organizational Dynamics* 3

(Autumn, 1974), pp. 3-17; *Inner Contradictions of Rigorous Research* (New York: Academic Press, 1980), p. 1.

   2. Argyris, *Personality and Organization*, p. 229.

   3. Chris Argyris, *The Applicability of Organizational Sociology* (New York: Cambridge University Press, 1974), pp. 67-72.

   4. Argyris, "Personality vs. Organization," p. 15; "Is Capitalism the Culprit?," *Organizational Dynamics* 6 (Spring, 1978), pp. 29-36; "Double Loop Learning In Organizations," *Harvard Business Review*, 55, 5 (Sept., 1977), pp. 115-126 et passim. Argyris' action orientation, much of it accomplished with Donald Shön, emerged in the early 1970s. This orientation studies what the individual "is capable of, not merely how he currently behaves." This focus on action research therefore has been directed to altering the status quo of organizational quality of life by seeking improvements in information processes in organizations. In this regard, his approach focuses on the study of organizational learning systems as "an ecological system of factors" that inhibit or facilitate learning activities of individuals.

   5. Argyris, *Inner Contradictions*, pp. 4-5.

   6. Ibid., p. 5. Argyris says that, "the old masters in sociology" -- Durkheim, Pareto, and Weber -- as well as "the old masters in psychology" -- McDougal, Freud and Lewin -- intertwined descriptive and normative views, and thus classical social science was "both theoretical and practical." In this context, Argyris recognizes that "the investigator is both an observer and change-maker."

   7. Ibid., pp. 9-10.

   8. Chris Argyris, *Organization of a Bank* (New Haven: Yale Labor and Management Center, 1954), p. 12.

   9. Argyris, *Inner Contradictions*, p. 10.

   10. Argyris, *Personality and Organization*, pp. 20-49.

   11. Ibid.

   12. Argyris, *Organization of a Bank*, pp. 10-12.

   13. Argyris, *Applicability of Organizational Sociology*, p. 65.

   14. Argyris, *Inner Contradictions*, p. 19.

   15. Argyris, *Management and Organizational Development*, p. 183; *Applicability of Organizational Sociology*, pp. 63-67 et passim.

   16. Russell Jacoby, *Social Amnesia: A Critique of Conformist Psychology from Adler to Laing* (Boston: Beacon Press, 1975).

   17. Argyris, *Personality and Organization*, p. 240.

   18. Theodore Adorno, quoted in Jacoby, *Social Amnesia*, pp. 63-64.

19. Argyris, *Organization of a Bank*, p. 11.

20. Ibid., pp. 8-14.

21. Argyris, *Applicability of Organizational Sociology*, pp. 185-186.

22. Argyris, *Management and Organizational Development*, pp. 185-186.

23. Argyris, *Personality and Organization*, p. 77.

24. Argyris, *On Organization of the Future*, p. 14.

25. Ibid, p. 22.

26. Argyris, *Personality and Organization*, pp. 62-77.

27. Argyris, *On Organization of the Future*, pp. 12-13.

28. Argyris, "Personality vs. Organization, p. 10.

29. Argyris, "Leadership, Learning,and Changing the Status Quo," p. 29.

30. Argyris, *Organization of the Future*, pp. 27-29.

31. Argyris, "Personality vs. Organization," p. 12.

32. Jacoby, *Social Amnesia*, p. 37.

33. Ibid., p. 34.

34. Ibid., p. 68.

35. Argyris, "Personality vs. Organization," p. 13.

36. Herbert G. Reid and Ernest J. Yanarella, "Critical Political Theory and Moral Development: Toward a Critical Phenomenological Outlook," Department of Political Science, University of Kentucky, paper delivered at the Midwest Political Science Convention, April, 1976, p. 10.

37. Jacoby, *Social Amnesia*, pp. 63-65.

38. Ibid., p. 65.

39. David Rasmussen, "Between Autonomy and Sociality," *Cultural Hermeneutics*, 1 (1973), pp. 8-9.

40. Ibid., pp. 20-21.

41. Ibid., p. 22.

42. Argyris, *Personality and Organization*, p. 242.

43. Jacoby, *Social Amnesia*, pp. 23-24.

44. Argyris, *Personality and Organization*, pp. 23-24.

45. Randall H. Ihara, *Confronting the Problem of Political Vision: Gabriel Marcel, Emmanuel Mounier and Chris Argyris* (University of Tennessee, unpublished Masters Thesis, 1970) p. 131.

46. Ibid., p. 132.

47. Ibid., pp. 133-135.

48. Chris Argyris, *Understanding Organizational Behavior* (Glencoe, Ill.: Dorsey Press, 1960), p. 10.

49. Denhardt, *Theories of Public Organization* (1984), p. 99.

50. Ibid., p. 99.

5

Criteria Considerations for Public Organization

The interpretative efforts of the previous chapters have illuminated how various models of contemporary organizations have failed to produce a paradigm of organization that can authentically be designated as "public." Therefore, the fundamental intent of this chapter, after a summary perspective of the issues of previous chapters, is to address criteria considerations envisioned as decisive for a model of organization that is more genuinely public.

REVIEW OF PREVIOUS CHAPTERS

Chapter 1 sought to demonstrate the importance of the administrative management orientation of Luther Gulick's views on organization in particular and administration in general. Particular attention was directed to elucidating the priority on efficient operations within Gulick's perspective. Not only does Gulick's view of organization provide an impetus to an administrative management understanding of organization, but also his organizational efficiency priority personifies an ideological conception or a reified conception of "efficiency." In this view, efficiency characterizes activity of coordination and control of specialized work functions under one ultimate center of authority. In other words, Gulick's reified efficiency or homogeneity is centered upon the design and accomplishments of organizational arrangements to permit the achievement of work in the most efficient fashion of management goals. Alternately, reified or ideological efficiency refers to the reduction of reason to instrumental modes of thinking and acting, modes that serve to mystify social relations in human consciousness. Moreover, efficiency is ideology because it confines efficiency to functional roles that humans assume in organizational life. Thus work experience prospects are therefore limited to what can be achieved merely within these functional tasks or roles.

Chapter 2 examined the administrative rational model of Herbert Simon. In Simon's perspective, the rationality of the organization is understood as synonymous with the efficiency of the administrative unit itself. Therefore, rationality or efficiency is a basic necessity for individuals as well as for management. In addition to efficiency as organizational rationality, Simon's view on organization has a central concern with decision making and its accompanying rationality as a limited or bounded process grounded in means-ends reasoning of individuals. Moreover, this reasoning process follows the organizational authority structure. Thus rational individual decision making takes place in conditions where the individual permits his or her choices to be guided by the decision premises of organizational superiors.

Decisions in Simon's model are identified as limited in the sense that humans "satisfice" instead of maximizing their choices. His view of satisficing entails looking for courses of action that are satisfactory or "good enough" given the limitations of time, cognitive ability, and so forth.

It was shown that this bounded rationality was a cognitive, means-ends process of the personal mind, whereby one matches one of various "means" to a "given end" as specified by administrative management. Both human choice and politics are restrictive matters of administrative management in Simon's model. Specifically, choice and politics are restricted to matters limited to administrative management. Alternately, the supremacy of rationality relegates values such as public, democracy, citizenship, and justice to secondary statuses.

Vincent Ostrom's democratic administration described in Chapter 3 was seen as a more humane and more democratic approach to organization than found in either Gulick's or Simon's perspectives. In fact, Ostrom's model is the antithesis of hierarchy and bureaucratic structures of authority. As previously noted, one major benefit of Ostrom's paradigm relates to its focus on individual opportunity rather than management's need for efficient operations. Additionally, Ostrom's model is based on dispersed and fragmented authority rather than centralized authority under one ultimate executive.

Nonetheless, Ostrom's model presents significant obstacles to the realization of a genuinely public organizational theory. The individualistic grounding of his model located in natural law and economic self-interest was shown to be an unlikely foundation for true public organization. Simply put, this foundation does not facilitate social consciousness. Rather, it encourages private consciousness, competition, and basic adaptation to existing social conditions. Similarly, his preference for constitutionalism as the fundamental authority structure for organization cannot enhance the prospects for political action as found in the writings of Sheldon Wolin, Kirk Thompson, and others. Completely absent in Ostrom's works are the social awareness of the institutional footing of meaning and the possibilities for participatory action needed for a theory of public organization.

Chapter 4 examined the primacy of self-development in the writings of Chris Argyris. This chapter, like the previous ones, offered a searching critique of establishing the groundwork of public organization on the individual. Although some of Argyris' assumptions have real value, his psychological self-development scheme is based philosophically in individualist morality and his perspective encompasses a view of organization as a system. At the same time, like Gulick, Simon's or Ostrom's perspectives, his organizational orientation is unable to promote social awareness of and common action in human problems shared in everyday organizational existence.

Argyris' political view on organization resides in the political philosophy of "new liberalism." He shows explicit and repeated preferences for administrative, over democratically political, problem solving. This is in harmony with the modern administrative outlook. Additionally, his orientation to leadership and existing power structure within organization is directly reflective of the new liberal outlook. This is especially apparent in Argyris' stand toward social reality. Traditionally, he addresses social or intersubjective conditions found in organizational life from a perspective of the existential self's needs of personality criteria. The problem of such a view is that it encounters difficulties trying to account for any impediments to human development inherent in social reality (vs. a reality restricted to the personal mind). It was pointed out that personal growth based in the inner or subjective self is unable to foster social awareness in others and hence prospects for social action. Thus development that is confined (as in Argyris' later works which move to a more interpersonal consideration of man) to individual health and well-being is a restrictive perspective on growth. Its greatest limitations lie in its lack of knowledge and avenues for action by which a person's political development can be equally fostered.

PUBLIC, DEMOCRATIC POLITICS AND CRITICAL ORGANIZATION RESEARCH

Noticeably absent also among the four organizational approaches of the theorists examined are democratic political values and processes as priorities of organization and particularly in the internal dimensions of organization. That is, conspicuous in their absence in Gulick's, Simon's, Ostrom's, and Argyris' orientations are explicit priorities on "democratic" values and processes which can directly promote employee policymaking or decision making in a democratic organizational life and for authentic "public" enterprise.

This situation is not only true with these four theorists, but it is quite evident generally throughout the literature on government administration, as the central focus is typically on "government" administration rather than "public" administration. Moreover, most administrative literature is confined to the "external" interactions of government organization via with other institutional actors, that is, Congress, the executive branch, clientele, and so on. Conversely, the literature on the internal aspects of organizations (which is relatively small in the government area compared to external studies) is almost explicitly concerned with bureaucratic management and hierarchical concerns of organizational elites. Typically, therefore, "public" or "publicness" are rare concerns, as such terms are almost always made to be synonyms for "government." Specifically, in such a scenario, public is assessed *within* the perimeters of the overall government institutional system. However, internal to particular government institutions themselves, there is little, if any, attention given to whether such processes are democratic or not.

In contemporary society, even conventional understandings of the term "politics" does not incorporate concepts of an active civic life, or a life of commonwealth, in society in general and certainly not in organizational life.[1] Moreover, this is especially true for government bureaucracies which typically label themselves as "public" administration structures or units. In contrast to the government bureaucracy view above, the traditional civic republican (or commonwealth) perspective views the aim of the public, especially government institutions or organizations, as a perspective that expresses "general" or common "understandings of the ends of social life and (seeks) to cultivate the kinds of practices that nurture those ends and the character of citizens."[2]

Indeed, William M. Sullivan has pointed out that the notion of the citizen is unintelligible apart from commonwealth, and long ago Aristotle showed how the concept of citizen cannot be considered apart from the concept of the common good or the common union. Accordingly, both of these demonstrate, Harry Boyte argues, that "we are by nature political beings,"[3] or political creatures in Aristotle's language, because the "meaning of the terms like 'people,' 'patriotic,' 'and sacred values'" can only be understood in context, from an analysis of who uses them."[4] Consequently, control over organizational decisions by bureaucratic structures and their authority in expertise and managers serves to undermine the public internal foundations of government organizations. Sullivan, drawing upon Alexis de Tocqueville's warning of "industrial feudalism," observes how "constraining administration serves to maintain private benefits, at least for some," but it does so at the price of truly public organization grounded in "genuine participation and self-determination."[5]

Thus a public organization is, according to Aristotle, one of common involvement or a common union, one based on shared needs or mutual interests expressed collectively in a "self-governing" association "of equals concerned about the general welfare." At base, therefore, public is *not* a euphemism; it is *not* a synonym for "government" organization. Specifically, public is not only characterized by politics, but particularly by a *democratic* conception of politics of the common or general good of citizens located internally, as well as externally, to the organization. It entails the political process that centers itself upon the shared values and processes of active citizens in the enterprise.

These dimensions are explicitly missing from the conceptualizations of Gulick, Simon, and Argyris and are found in only a modified form in Ostrom's individualism. But in all the organizational theorists examined, the notion of public, common, or general involvement is absent. Public involvement or public action expressly is needed for a public organization. Furthermore, public action is that which originates in the common or general goals of all people of the organization or all participants. This is so because only common action "promises genuine progress toward administrative praxis or self-creating public action which transcends forces outside of human control in contemporary administered societies."[6]

This view on the public is consistent with and originates in the concept noted both here and in the Introduction. This is a view found in the works of Aristotle, Cicero, Sheldon Wolin, Brian Fay, Harry Boyte, William Sullivan, and many others. So organizational theories that place central importance on these attributes of the public are theories that are consistent with traditional and western democratic theory.

On the level of organizational research, the achievement of a theory of public organization involves a radical critique of knowledge as social theory. The work of Dunn and Fozouni, their synthesizing and analyzing the works of Habermas, Max Horkheimer, Paul Lazarfield and other theorists, shows how such critical research is well within the scope of the social sciences because the "knowledge-constitution of critical sciences is emancipatory."[7] Moreover, in observing the "totality as well as its historical dynamics, critical theory" also extends to specialized areas such as public administration. In other words, while the critical sciences' "overarching research interest is emancipation,"[8] it is also concerned with the hermeneutic and technical aspects of knowledge. Specifically, critical administrative research "mediates the interpretative understanding of a way of life." Simultaneously, it is also focused on "technical interests which underlie the extension of power of technical control in increasingly large and complex organization."[9]

An equally important concern of critical social analysis is that it enhances self-reflection through critiques of ideology. Critiques of ideology are especially applicable toward the different uses of science and technology in contemporary organizational society. Ideology critiques are especially helpful "for reflecting critically on the interests which guide the production and use of knowledge in different disciplines." Furthermore, self-reflection enables one "to understand human interests *underlying* knowledge [my emphasis], an understanding for a society in which 'rationality,'" as Habermas originally noted, "is no longer confined to pre-scientific and ideological assumptions of various sciences."

In a broader context, the critique of ideology, whether used in research or the practice of life, "provides the only satisfactory framework for the growth of knowledge in a society committed to human emancipation.[10]

Therefore, the investigations covered in the work of Gulick, Simon, Ostrom, and Argyris employed the critical approach as the essential mode of analysis. The critical perspective was used to expose the ideological bases in various organizational theories. Namely, ideological concerns were exposed by situating the notions of the public, citizenship, and public organization in their historical settings and by elucidating how such traditionally political notions have been transformed over time.

TOWARD PUBLIC ORGANIZATION: CRITERIA CONSIDERATIONS

The second task of this chapter is to outline the key features of a more genuine model of public organization. Such a model is approached in terms of the criteria envisioned as basic to self-creating public action.

The organizational perspectives of Chapter 1-4 were selected for analysis because each scholar's work represented and exemplified a major subdisciplinary realm found in the literature of public administration.

In the analyses of Gulick's, Simon's, Ostrom's, and Argyris' views, it was shown that each theorist's work fails to provide for organization based on general participation needed for public action. This is because each theorist submerges collaborative involvement in favor of what he sees as more primary concerns. Thus the most fundamental criterion necessary for self-creating public action is absent in each theorist's perspective.

Not only was each theorist's conceptual priority investigated, but each chapter entailed critically interpreting how historical and theoretical developments found in the writings of each theorist were influenced by the larger social totality. This entails critically analyzing, in each theorist's works, two interrelated dimensions of influence on their thoughts. First, this included investigating historically specific influences on scholar's work. Second, the location of their respective historical outlooks in the structure of political economy were examined. In other words, the critical investigation on these two analytical levels across the four chapters illuminates why a depoliticized and a depublicized value emphasis is found in each writer's model.

For example, the general neglect of emphasis on the public and politics results from the cultural and ideological ramifications of managerialism and from economic and psychological individualism. Second, the location of the respective historical outlooks within the structure of political economy was examined.

Since Gulick, Simon, Ostrom, and Argyris offer perspectives with inadequate conceptual groundings for public organization, alternate criteria are required for true public action, that is, action originating in common or mutual goals that emerge from general organization participation. Such criteria are found in *democracy*, *sociality*, and *psychopolitical development*. First, for example, a more genuine public organization is based in participatory democracy as the guiding social ethic of organization. Hence the fundamental value or priority in organization, in the critical model, rests with politics, not with administration. Second, a more critically public organization model is grounded in the everyday lifeworld's modes of dialectical sociality. That is, organizational participants place emphasis on mutual reciprocity, on shared or mutual concerns and needs, over private or purely material aspects of humans. Third, the more public organizational paradigm recognizes the importance of comprehensive human development, which is essential for reinforcing and sustaining democratic participation. While the more critical model is indeed concerned with the personal growth of individuals, it transcends this limited form of development for a more comprehensive development equally concerned with promoting the person's political and social participation in the organization. The criteria of democracy as participation, sociality, and comprehensive, that is, psychopolitical, development are examined more closely in later sections.

DEMOCRACY AS THE GUIDING SOCIAL ETHIC OF ORGANIZATION

Public organizations are recognized as "historically created, humanly derived institutions, always subject to analysis and reformulation." Additionally, Robert B. Denhardt suggests that in public organizations individuals "would be seen as *active* participants in the process of constructing and modifying these institutions."[11] Because a fundamental aspect of public organization is that it "permits possibilities for growth, creativity and indeed *choice* for individuals' everyday life experiences in organizational settings."[12] The predominant value concept of social interaction found in Gulick, Simon, Ostrom, and Argyris does not promote this dimension of public organization. Rather, potential for the realization of public organization requires a fundamental or guiding social ethic, which is provided by democratic participatory politics in the critical model.

This priority on democratic participation entails awareness of humans as "social beings," as persons with social as well as personal needs. This participation, which focuses on humans both individually and collectively, is clearly at odds with theories that envision humans as essentially instruments of management or mere mechanisms of the market. In the democratic politics of participation, humans are recognized as beings rooted in concrete social experiences of everyday existence. They are thus conceived simultaneously as both objects and subjects of organization, that is, say they help fashion the organization "by their own choices and actions, and by their responses"[13] to the organization as an ongoing process. Moreover, the "process character of participation has a built-in safeguard. It encourages a continuing reassessment of previous outcomes."[14] Therefore, the experience of participation, according to Bachrach and Botwinick, "usually fosters" the self-development of participants while "promoting communal values."[15] The fostering of communal values is essential for true public organization. Action follows values and, Denhardt points out, "the values of the organization must be subject to debate and deliberation by those throughout the organization." Furthermore, values "selected in a less public process are simply not likely to endure."[16]

The politics of democratic participation as the guiding ethic is therefore a commitment necessary for creating and sustaining actions/decisions that qualify as *public*. Participation involves creative inter-

action. In other words, creative interaction entails collaboration needed for self-creating public action or action expressing common goals
of the organization. In short, participation or collaboration is the application of "civic virtue"[17] to the everyday work life of organization.

Another prominent theorist who has elaborated the importance of
this type of political decision making is Brian Fay. Fay shows that
collaborative decision making cannot be limited to the end results that
are produced by participation. Indeed, like Pateman, Bachrach and
Botwinick, and others, Fay recognizes that essential virtue in participation is attached to "the process by which such authoritative decisions are made." More specifically, participatory democracy is centered on peoples' "deliberate efforts to order, direct and control *their
own* [my emphasis] collective affairs and activities" within the organization's daily work situations.[18]

Thus the politics of democratic participation is essential not only
for prospects for self-creating public action, that is, administrative praxis. It is also necessary for personal self-reflection and hence freedom.
For example, Fay remarks:

> men are self-conscious creatures who can reflect on their
> experiences and actions and on the arrangements by which
> they can order their lives, and who can, on the basis of this
> self-reflection, change the way they live: human conscious-
> ness thus implies a process of self-formation in which new
> forms of experience and action are made possible because
> one has reflected on his past experience.[19]

Thus participatory political activity "must be understood as the same
process undertaken by members of the group" or organization "with
respect to their group identity" because such politics is to collective
affairs of organization "what the strivings for autonomy is to personal
matters." Therefore, Fay suggests, it is for this reason that humans
"can be free only when they participate in determining the conditions
of their own lives." That is, they can be free only when they are "not
simply subject to the commands of others." This is so, he adds, because to be "deprived of the opportunites to participate is to lose the
chance to exercise one's own power of self-reflection." In addition,
one therefore loses the essential human capacity of self-determination
"with regard to some of the most important areas of our existence."

Thus one can be genuinely free only when one posseses the capacity to be self-determining.[20]

SOCIALITY

In contrast to purely materialistic renderings of human existence where managerial perspectives dominate organization, or where private economics and other calculated "interests" are ultimately rooted in the possessive self, the critical perspective on public organization is premised on humans as thoroughly social beings.

This understanding of the human as a social creature as found in the more authentic public model has been articulated lucidly in the work of David Rasmussen. The assumption that humans are fundamentally social beings recognizes that his "is not something freely chosen by the actor on the social scene." Rather, he says, "social identity must be conceived as the ground of self-identity" because humans emerge on the social scene "neither as pure consciousness nor as individual selves but as a social self with a social identity."[21] Rasmussen goes on to point out how the self is, indeed, a social self psychologically, philosophically, and sociologically. In other words, this is valid in the psychological sense where "self-definition is a resolution of desire for the other and the simultaneous need for the other's recognition." It is also "true in a philosophical sense inasmuch as it is through the recognition given and established to the self that the self comes to know itself as a self." It is also true "in a sociological sense because it is through these modes of institutional identity" created by society that the self "comes to *be* as a self."[22] Consequently, the critical understanding of people as thoroughly social creatures permits cognizance "of ourselves as expressions of the institutions in which we live and work rather than conceiving of ourselves as something distinct from them."[23]

The more critical public organization model does indeed acknowledge the necessity of material existence. Yet such needs are mediated by necessities of nonmaterial existence. In a word, this theory recognizes the legitimacy of basic social needs and other commonly ascertained dimensions of the people in organizational situations. These dimensions also include those needs, aspirations, feelings, and so on of a personal nature. So in this model of organization the material, non-material, social, as well as personal desires and needs are recognized as primarily met through public action. And public action is arrived at through participation and is made possible through the understanding provided by sociality.

Sociality, it will be recalled, was discussed in various aspects in Chapter 3 and particularly in Chapter 4. By way of brief review, the perspective provided by sociality elucidates an individual's relationship to other humans (and nonhuman nature) as one of intersubjective relatedness. In other words, one shares an inter-subjective relatedness in common everyday existence. Put simply, man's relationship to others is dialectical: humans are mutually reciprocal in their interactions with others.

Furthermore, the sociality perspective understands humans as essentially active and social rather than passive and atomistic. Michael Harmon, for instance, expresses this fundamental dialectic succinctly. He says that people "have a measure of autonomy in determining their actions." At the same time, such actions are "bound-up in a social context, i.e., in the presence of others." Also, according to Harmon, this "social context is necessary not only for instruction purposes but also it defines people's status as human."[24] The understanding of the relationship between people and social reality provided by the life-world structures of sociality reinforce and are reinforced by democratic politics as the ethic of organization. This can be illustrated, for example, by Brian Fay's comments on how participatory political activity emphasizes man's social character and, conversely, how social self-consciousness engenders, in turn, political action. He points out that the ideas people have of the social world, as well as what is "right and fitting," of what their abilities are, as well as what they are worth and what they ought to aspire to, are all "ideas which comprise men's images of themselves." Moreover, all of these originate in the social world where people live. Fay notes that humans become self-conscious through the process of becoming members of a social order, by learning its language, by adopting the standards of excellence of the social order, and through comparing themselves to others. In other words:

> What each person is results in large part from what others think him to be. It is because of this aspect of human consciousness that politics, argument, persuasion and actions

are thought to be fundamental aspects of human life, for it is in these sorts of activities that men self-consciously reveal themselves to others and in the process learn who they are and what they want. Political life is thus an indispensable process of becoming and being a person.[25]

PSYCHOPOLITICAL DEVELOPMENT

The understanding of sociality as a structural foundation to the everyday intersubjective life-world, along with understanding "intentionality grounded embodied ego,"[26] provide a grounding for human development in a more authentic model of public organization. That is, sociality and embodied ego permit a psychopolitical mode of human development applicable to everyday, intersubjective life. These univeral structures of common interpersonal existence permit a development where identity, individuality, autonomy, and the human self are recognized as thoroughly social and possessing the ongoing processes of existential becoming in the context of political activity. In psychopolitical development, therefore, identity, autonomy, and so forth are socially earned and continually re-earned through political participatory activity. In short, people participate with others to meet social, as well as personal needs or to reform, or even to reconstruct, social organization. This is a political activity that emerges from and is applicable to the most basic dimension of human life. Specifically, it is applicable to the *Lebenswelt* or "life-world" of intersubjective, multilevel everyday existence we all inhabit in common as social creatures through and through.[27]

Thus the criterion of psychopolitical development is vital for a more critically public organization perspective inasmuch as such development prospects make democratic participation practical. As such, this type of growth is essential for administrative praxis. Moreover, the ultimate realization of participatory politics in organizational settings and subsequently public action is contingent upon the growth of humans psychopolitically in their concrete intersubjective situations.

Psychopolitical development was earlier described as concerned with personal, political, and social growth. It is also focused on enhancing understanding among human actors in the everyday organizational existence. Therefore, it is a mode of growth that seeks to present human actors with an understanding that transcends the limitations discussed with self-development's thrust on individualist subjectivity and morality. By acknowledging man's fundamental social nature, it simultaneously recognizes the necessity of social action for addressing both the social and objective conditions posed by organizational realities, that is, particularly those conditions that are themselves constructed out of past, present, and future actions.

In some ways, self-development and psychopolitical development are alike. Both modes of development acknowledge the legitimacy of the psychological needs of human actors. This includes essential personal requisites in both the affective and competence realms of the human psyche. However, unlike self-development, the mode of psychopolitical development is not grounded in the internal or inner self of autonomous man. Rather, the life-world structures of psychopolitical growth mediate a tacit subjectivity with cognizance of objective reality. The human actor is thus understood as a being formed by and continually socialized in the social environment, and yet as a being who actively and/or passively gives form to that environment. People are therefore provided understanding of how they are simultaneously determining agents on, as well as being persons influenced by, their respective conditions and daily situations. Furthermore, participants gain such understanding through reflection made possible by their awareness of their own social nature. In other words, by participants' understanding of others for definition of their own selves, or, as Rasmussen explains, "through the discovery of a socialized identity, the groundwork for a reflection which is transformative is provided.[28]

In psychopolitical development, prospects for human reflection are thereby made possible insofar as organizational participants are able to make distinctions between their "institutional identity" and their "postulated desire."[29] Put simply, human actors are able to recognize they exist in a cultural life-world that is "already determined" and that this life-world's institutions bestow contingent identities and otherwise determine their lives. On the other hand, this determination is "a determination in time so it is a determination that can be overcome"[30] because psychopolitical development's foundation in sociality provides humans with the recognition that everyday institutions or organizations are historical, that is, manmade, products. In a word, they are humanly derived and socially created. Therefore they are open to social transformation through mutual or shared cooperation, effort, or action.

Hence psychopolitical development is to be understood as a key to the long-term institutionalization of the legitimacy of democratic participation needed for truly public work life. This occurs because such development fosters the social authority basis required to make organizational forms practical in the larger culture over time. In other words, the social authority emerging from widespread participation facilitates participation's appearance in other aspects of society. Thus over the long-term this development legitimates the ethic of democracy into a commitment in everyday life and in the physical-geographical areas of most localized human concerns. These areas are the particular situations and social conditions faced by ordinary humans in organizations.

NOTES

1. Harry Boyte, *Commonwealth: A Return to Citizen Politics* (New York: The Free Press, 1989), p. xxi.

2. Sullivan. *Reconstructing Public Philosophy*, p. 59.

3. Boyte, *Commonwealth*, p. 8.

4. Ibid., p. 33.

5. Sullivan, *Reconstructing Public Philosophy*, pp. 7-8 et passim.

6. Dunn and Fozouni, *Toward a Critical Administrative Theory*, p. 62.

7. Ibid., p. 60.

8. Ibid., p. 61.

9. Ibid., p. 61.

10. Ibid., p. 61. Dunn and Fozouni quote from Jurgen Habermas, *Knowledge and Human Interests* (Boston: Beacon Books, 1971).

11. Robert B. Denhardt, *In the Shadow of Organization* (Lawrence: Regents Press of Kansas, 1981), p. 73.

12. Ibid., p. 63.

13. Pranger, *Eclipse of Citizenship*, p. 92.

14. Bachrach and Botwinick, *Power and Empowerment*, p. 28.

15. Ibid, p. 29

16. Denhardt, *The Pursuit of Significance*, p. 31.

17. Pranger, *Eclipse of Citizenship*, pp. 50-53.

18. Fay, *Social Theory and Political Practice*, p. 54.

19. Ibid.

20. Ibid.

21. Rasmussen, "Between Autonomy and Sociality," pp. 41-42.

22. Ibid., p. 42.

23. Ibid., p. 20.

24. Harmon, *Action Theory for Public Administration*, p. 31.

25. Fay, *Social Theory and Political Practice*, p. 55.

26. Through the intentionality of purposes the embodied ego, via tacit subjectivity, develops through a "living cohesion." The embodied self experiences itself while belonging to the world and others. Thus embodied ego is recognition of human subjectivity as social and institutional in context. See John O'Neil, quoted in Reid and Yanarella, "Critical Political Theory," pp. 19-20.

27. Ibid., p. 25.

28. Rasmussen, *Cultural Hermeneutics*, p. 43.

29. Ibid., pp. 42-43.

30. Ibid., p. 43.

Appendix:
The Expansion of the
Public Sphere

I began this work by observing the axiom in political theory that theory informs practice; that values inform actions. It is therefore reasonable, as well as pertinent, to ask if or what evidence is available as to whether organizations can be made more democratically participatory and thus more public for its members. In response to such a question, it can be empirically shown, in both private and government realms, that organizations can indeed be made more democratic for its members and that the public sphere can be opened.

Across western industrial societies of North America and Western Europe, a body of literature has developed over the past three decades which indicate that organizations can be and are being made more internally and externally public. First, in the area of workplace democratization, studies illuminate the internal dynamics and the fostering of citizenship within the organization. Other research shows how government organizations internally, as well as externally, can and are opening the public spheres to everyday members of the greater society.

First, the democratization of internal organizational structure has been taking place for more than thirty years in private industries in Europe and in the United States. Peter Bachrach and Aryeh Botwinick recently argued

> participation is an indispensable component of a healthy
> democratic polity. This is so as in the absense of such

> participation, leaders become unresponsive to the needs of
> the people.[1]

This holds for the larger societal polity but it also holds for members of organizations as polities in their own right. The democratization of the internal organizational structure has been, as noted, occurring in American and European industries for more than three decades. This democratization has been in diverse types of industries with various forms of processes and structures modified marginally to suit different needs. These are typically designated as participatory democracy, workplace democratization, industrial democracy, workers' self-management, self-governing enterprises, or other similar labels. A substantial body of literature in the social sciences is available on this phenomenon and has been since the late 1960s and early 1970s. Moreover, while this literature follows domestic efforts, it also echoes an established tradition of workplace democratization already established for some time in Europe.

Empirical and theoretical studies undertaken on the workplace democracy phenomenon are quite numerous. Among some of the prominent studies are those of Paul Bernstein[2], Paul Blumberg[3], Gerry Hunnius, G. David Garson and John Case[4], David Jenkins[5], Robert Dahl[6], Carole Pateman[7], and Edward Greenburg.[8] The literature on workplace democratization demonstrates that organization can indeed be structured so as to be democratically responsive to member input on policymaking. Thus members become citizens of the organization, internal to it, they become collaborators or policymakers of the organizational agenda. That is, the organization takes on a character of a humanly derived association based in the common good of the organization. Moreover, it is a common good established by the workers themselves in shared or mutual effort.

For more germane prospects in the realm of government and society in general, empirical evidence is also present on efforts to open the public sphere societywide or for generally opening the government realm of society. These studies also originate in the mid-1970s and reflect research on opening the public realm of existence in Germany (formerly West Germany), Sweden, Denmark, the Netherlands, and other nations of Western Europe.

Significantly, these studies show that efforts to open the public sphere not only did so but also they transcended traditional bureaucratic modes of organizing in moving to new levels of organization. Indeed, an interesting side observation from such research is that evidence illuminates that bureaucracy is not, nor need it be, accepted as "the" only structure and rationality for organization. Besides showing practical alternatives to bureaucracy, these studies on opening the public spheres readily illuminate ways government organizations can be made more responsive to the common, general or public good.

The identification of practical avenues for extending public involvement is a necessary and crucial concern for the realization of the critical model of public organization. Traditional organizations are formed around the delivery of services or they are concerned with a particular policy area. Consequently, participants in policymaking processes of the organizations of which they are members are restricted in their membership. Furthermore, in the vast majority of circumstances, decision-making or substantive policy input is actually limited to an organizational elite of management and/or specialists. Therefore, in order to open the public sphere and public participation in organizational policy formation (and actual decision-making capabilities) requires methods that will extend involvement beyond a select technical or managerial few. Three cross-national studies, in particular, by Leon Lindberg[9], Dorothy Nelkin[10], and Mans Lonnroth[11] address this issue in various situations. Their research illuminates a variety of national experiments that have been implemented in various European industrialized nations to expand public participation.

One of these nations, on which all these scholars have done research, is Sweden. Originally with respect to energy, but today in various other issue areas, Sweden has used a variety of experimental efforts to increase public involvement within and between government operations. While each of the three scholars notes the experimental nature of these efforts to expand the public realm, the research evidence nonetheless demonstrates how the public sphere has been significantly enlarged in Sweden. Furthermore, such examples are indicative of how widespread collaboration can be practically applied in a complex, industrialized nation. Their research also shows how participation has been successfully undertaken in contemporary settings and on issues usually considered highly complex and technical.

Specifically, these efforts to increase participation provide vivid empirical illustrations of how Sweden has tried to extend the influence exerted by the public realm toward differing energy and environmental issues facing that society.[12] Moreover, this expansion of citizen and public involvement is shown to be promoted literally by the government of Sweden. One of the methods entailed in this enterprise consisted of the initiation of "public education and consultation"[13] in Sweden's energy policy. Expansion of the public sphere has also occurred by government's attempt "to introduce ways to increase local participation in physical planning."[14] In addition, other efforts to broaden participation in decisions concerning scientific research and development have also taken place.[15]

The efforts to secure more direct public collaboration on the specific issue of energy policy in Sweden made use of "study circles." These represented a system of small study groups managed by political parties and the major popular organizations (trade unions, temperance groups and religious groups) and financed principally by government funds.[16] According to Nelkin, "over half the adult population is estimated to belong to these popular movements."[17]

Until a little after mid-century, Sweden did not possess a gestalt energy policy per se. Rather, before the 1950s the nation's policy concerns were based on electricity policy, fuel (wood and peat), and so forth. However, with the emergence of nuclear power, fuel and electricity became one energy issue. This situation occured because technological change, as Lonnroth points out, "held out the possibility of merging two hitherto separate technical supply systems and that made electricity economically competitive with fuel for space heating."[18] Yet by the 1970s, controversies over health and safety issues associated with nuclear power, as well as widespread opposition among the population to further construction of nuclear plants,[19] compelled the government to seek ways to expand involvement of the public in nuclear decisions. At the same time, during the 1950s to 1970s period, Sweden, like other western nations, was becoming increasingly dependent on foreign oil. In the oil embargo of 1973-74, Sweden's vulnerability to external powers in this area was well exposed.

This situation precipitated a review of energy policy in the Swedish parliament on both nuclear and oil policy. Thus these events triggered the government's efforts in sponsoring the study groups or "study circles" campaign.

The energy study groups began in earnest in 1974; initially some 8,000 study circles were set up, with more than 80,000 participants. Furthermore, the government's decision to sponsor study circles in the field "reflected an open recognition that this area," which was normally "considered only within the Ministries and most in terms of technical questions, should be discussed from diverse ideological perspectives."[20]

In a specific breakdown of participants and costs, Dorothy Nelkin has noted:

> The organizations were invited to participate and seven accepted; the LO (the major union) ran 3000 circles; the ABF (run by Social Democrats) sponsored 4500 circles; two Folk Schools (run by the Center and Liberal parties) sponsored 2000 each; the Conservatives sponsored 500; and adult education groups run by temperance movements of the Church of Sweden organized several hundred others. Each circle had between ten and fifteen members and met together for at least ten hours. . . . The Ministries of Education train leaders, recruit participants, and develop their own materials in addition to what was provided by government. The entire costs of the program came to about $650,000.[21]

Nelkin also points out that the study circles covered several questions and "that each was determined in the context of political choice." Additionally, "the study of material, as well as the procedures for discussions, differed greatly among the organizers."[22]

Similarly, Lonnroth has noted that, while the debate on energy centered around nuclear power, it later took on new dimensions. It became a debate on "how much energy was needed, and what the relationships were between energy supply and different social goals such as high employment, welfare, environmental questions and so forth . . . the debate rapidly evolved into fundamental political views on society."[23] Therefore, what has been a decision-making process involving only highly competent and specialized technocrats, before the 1974 period, was "taken out of their hands and put squarely in the range of issues that are influenced at the political level."[24]

Inroads have also been made in Sweden to increase local participation in physical planning. For example, the Swedish Ministries of Communes "offered to pay for any experiments in participation by municipal governments." There followed "a series of efforts" by scientists, architects, and the public through exhibits of plans and through public discussion. Moreover, "some local governments set up consultative procedures with local area councils and popular associations." Also, more recent proposals "have included the creation within communities of smaller neighborhoods, each with special councils to discuss local issues.[25] Among other areas pointed out by Nelkin where public involvement has been expanded by Sweden's efforts to democratize various policy and organizational processes are education, scientific research, and development.[26]

As these examples illustrate, an outline of a more critical model of public organization can indeed be found in everyday life and historical examples. These participatory experiments anticipate features of a critical model in various aspects of the operation of a more public organizational model. Simultaneously, these experiments have demonstrated how the public can be successfully expanded on a national level.

PUBLIC AND BUREAUCRATIC MODELS OF ORGANIZATION

The realization of a more authentically public organization model requires radically different human awareness and action orientations to organization-as-a-phenomenon than is typically found in contemporary culture. The critical model stands in vivid contrast to the prevalent bureaucratic model. This is especially true in the structural components or its social action mechanisms. At the same time, the political conditions or policies generated by the more genuinely public organization theory vary considerably from those of the bureaucratic model. For example, formal hierarchical structures of authority do not permit, let alone facilitate, psychopolitical development among workers. Nor do current hierarchical arrangements maximize public involvement and thus expansion of the public sphere of organizational existence. Additionally, decision-making components in the dominant bureaucratic model of organization categorically do not allow for open debate on policies nor even consideration of alternate policies by the general membership.

In this final section, varying dimensions for a more genuine public paradigm are outlined. This is presented in the schematic comparing and contrasting features of the formal bureaucratic model to the proposed critical paradigm. I then summarize specific standards by which the critical model can be evaluated.

COMPARISION OF TWO MODELS
OF ORGANIZATION

Dimension 1: Nature of Organization and Composition

Prevalent Bureaucratic Model

Organization is understood as a reified instrument of mechanical parts. The composition is conceived essentially as functionaries or dependents of managerial leadership/control.

Critical Model

Organization is a human social enterprise, a historically derived association. Composition is understood as human with each person a citizen of the organization.

It requires conditions that provide continually for political education such as the study circles observed in Sweden's efforts. In the critical model, such study groups could be employed not only to address intra- or interorganizational policies on goods and services provided by the organization. These groups would also function fundamentally in practice as a dynamic educational process in participatory politics. In this sense, employees learn of organization as a human field of their everyday work life. Such understanding promotes cognizances of work environments as a primary and right and proper realm of democratic citizenship.

Critical Model (cont.)

This requires political conditions that provide for continual political education. Such education is a prerequisite for encouraging understanding of the public sphere and is also essential for fostering mutual and individual political/psychological development. It encourages understanding of reality as manmade and politically alterable by social effort.

Dimension 2: Authority Structure of Organization

Prevalent Bureaucratic Model

The authority structure of bureaucracy is hierarchical. Interaction between persons is based in position status and characterized by obedience and passivity to managerially imposed objectives.

Critical Model

The authority structure is based in democracy. Interaction is characterized by open discussion among employees. This opportunity at freewheeling exchange of perception, and views on issues (presented by social conditions faced by employees in the work environment) facilitates participation. Hence democratic authority enhances opportunities for expanding/maintaining the public sphere within the organization. This authority is vital for promoting participation among equals. Also, it is necessary to engender an environment within which employees can pursue

Critical Model (cont.)

political, social, and personal development.

Dimension 3: Decision-Making in Organization

Prevalent Bureaucratic Model	*Critical Model*

Internal to Organization decision making rests with management and/or technical expertise. External organizational policy is also a function of administrative management in lieu of varying levels of influence as exerted by different aspects from other political institutions (i.e., impact of legislature, executive, courts, and relevant "groups" in society which bear on an organization's policy concerns).

Each person is a policy maker in organization. The nature of organization, its composition, and democratic authority structure which promotes participation makes each person a decision maker in collaboration with others. These previously noted political components democratize the organizational environment to permit equal input (one man, one vote) on policy decisions. Thus the criterion for participation in policy decisions is neither position status in the hierarchy nor technical expertise, but citizenship (membership) in the organization.

Policies affecting the population of society in general, or upon other organizations, beyond the service or product of the organization are subject to input by these outside influences. For example, for those affected directly by an organization's decisions (either people in general or other organizations), agreements could be secured allotting others an im-

Critical Model (cont.)

pact on one organization or vice versa. A certain percentage of an organization's decision-making capacity could be allotted to others generally or members affected in other organizations. As such, the ratio of organizational members (a constant) to members of the generally affected public (or members of other organizations) could be fixed or fluctuating across organizations or specific policy areas.

Dimension 4: Conflict Resolution

Prevalent Bureaucratic Model

In bureaucratic organization, conflict resolution is resolved by managerial control over the work force by appeal to status position, rules, coercion, demotion, dismissal, failure to acknowledge a difference exists, etc.

Critical Model

Conflict, like cooperation, is recognized as an aspect of collaborative interaction. As such, conflict is understood as a basic dimension of reality. Conflict is seen as subject to negotiation provided by the nature of the organization, its composition, and its authority structure. That is, conflict is subject to negotiation in an open atmosphere where trust can be established, differences reconciled, and solutions reached. This occurs through free, open expression and dialogue among conflicting parties.

Dimension 5: Human Development

Prevalent Bureaucratic Model   *Critical Model*

Development, to the extent accepted, in generally restricted to personal cognitive and emotional growth and interpersonal skills applicable directly to the organization's needs as defined by management.

Development is recognized to be not only psychological/emotional and social, but political as well. Each dimension is necessary to promote personal choice, creativity, freedom, self-reflection, and social responsibility needed for participation in public action.

Dimension 6: Leadership and Competence

Prevalent Bureaucratic Model   *Critical Model*

Management is leadership. Competence is in the function-role position or in expertise or specialization.

Leadership is by democratic election of fellow organizational members, subject to rotation or recall or both. Competence in the critical model is both personal and social. It is social insofar as competence is seen as the ability to work with and through others for the common good or the welfare of the self and others. It is personal in acknowledging the differences in taste, experiences, knowledge, and preferences among individuals.

Therefore, there are several criteria by which the critical model of public organization can be assessed. The most fundamental evaluative criteria include:

(a)   the critical organization provides participatory mechanisms by which all employees have the opportunities for political education;

(b)   in the critical organizational model, each human employee is a citizen of the organization;

(c)   this organization's authority structure is grounded thoroughly in democracy;

(d)   organizational policymakers in the critical model include each employee with final policy as an outcome of the democratic process;

(e)   the development of human members in the critical model of public organization is toward each person's total or whole being in its social, personal, and political dimensions; and,

(f)   the organization's leadership is chosen democratically by the members of the organization and those affected by its decisions.

NOTES

1. Bachrach and Botwinick, *Power and Empowerment,* p. 23.

2. Paul Bernstein, *Workplace Democratization* (New Brunswick, N.J.: Transaction Books, 1983).

3. Paul Blumberg, *Industrial Democracy: The Sociology of Participation* (New York: Schocken Books, 1968).

4. Gerry Hunnius, G. David Garson, and John Case, *Workers Control: A Reader on Labor and Social Change* (New York: Random House, 1973).

5. David Jenkins, *Job Power: Blue and White Collar Democracy* (New York: Penguin, 1974).

6. Robert A. Dahl, *A Preface to Economic Democracy* (Berkeley: University of California Press, 1985).

7. Carole Pateman, *Participation and Democratic Theory* (Cambridge: Cambridge University Press, 1970).

8. Edward Greenburg, *Workplace Democracy: The Political Effects of Participation* (Ithaca: Cornell University Press, 1986).

9. Leon N. Lindberg, ed., *The Energy Syndrome* (Lexington, Mass.: Lexington Books, 1977).

10. Dorothy Nelkin, *Technological Decisions and Democracy: European Experiments in Public Participation* (Beverly Hills: Sage Publications, 1977).

11. Mans Lonnroth, "Swedish Energy Policy: Technology in the Process," in Lindberg, *The Energy Syndrome*, pp. 255-283.

12. Public sphere concerns for the environment in Sweden differ noticeably from popular interest in environmental movements in the United States. Swedish public involvement is more accurately an ecological or ecosystem approach to nature than simply an orientation on environmentalism. As such, it is more condusive to promoting expansion of the public sphere than is the interest-group mentality of environmentalism in the United States. In the United States, environmentalism has been an interest-group phenomenon "weighted down by middle-class moralism and the culture of professionalism." In Sweden, by contrast, concerns for the environment and energy are tied to other concerns such as high employment, welfare, and various other facets of the natural and social systems. Therefore, environmental concerns in Sweden are more truly approached from a public ecological perspective in which natural and social concerns are seen as interrelated to other concerns. Ernest J. Yanarella vividly presents the fundamental differences between the ecological and environmental orientations toward nature. Moreover, he presents a lucid perspective on the prospects that each movement offers for contributing to progressive political change. See his "Environmental vs. Ecological Perspectives on Acid Rain: The American Environmental Movement and the West German Green Party," in *The Acid Rain Debate: Scientific, Economic and Political Dimensions* (Boulder, Colo.: Westview Press, 1985), pp. 243-260.

13. Nelkin, *Technological Decisions and Democracy*, p. 60.

14. Ibid., p. 64.

15. Ibid., p. 65.

16. Ibid., pp. 60-61.

17. Ibid., p. 20.

18. Lonnroth, "Swedish Energy Policy," p. 258.

19. Ibid., p. 269.

20. Nelkin, *Technological Decisions and Democracy*. pp. 43.

21. Ibid., pp. 61-62.

22. Ibid.
23. Lonnroth, "Swedish Energy Policy," pp. 258-259.
24. Ibid., p. 259.
25. Nelkin, *Technological Decisions and Democracy*, pp. 65-67.
26. Ibid., pp. 66-69.

Bibliography

Argyris, Chris. *The Applicability of Organizational Sociology.* New York: Cambridge University Press, 1974.

___. "Double Loop Learning in Organization." *Harvard Business Review* 55, 5 (September, 1977): 115-126.

___. *Inner Contradictions of Rigorous Research.* New York: Academic Press, 1980.

___. "Is Capitalism the Culprit?" *Organizational Dynamics* 6 (Spring, 1978): 29-36.

___. "Leadership, Learning and Changing the Status Quo." *Organizational Dynamics* 4, 3 (Winter, 1976): 29-43.

___. *Management and Organizational Development.* New York: McGraw Hill, 1971.

___. *On Organization of the Future.* Beverly Hills: Sage Professional Paper, Administrative and Policy Series no. 03-006, 1973.

___. *Organization of a Bank.* New Haven: Yale Labor and Management Center, 1954.

___. *Personality and Organization.* New York: Harper and Row, 1957.

___. "Personality vs. Organization." *Organizational Dynamics* 3 (Autumn, 1974): 3-17.

___. *Understanding Organizational Behavior.* Glencoe, Ill: Dorsey Press, 1960.

___, and Shön, Donald. *Action Theory in Practice: Increasing Professional Effectiveness.* San Francisco: Jossey-Bass, 1974.

Aristotle. *The Politics*. Rev. ed., translated by T.A. Sinclair, revised and represented by Trevor Saunders. New York: Penguin Books, 1981.

Bachrach, Peter, and Botwinick, Aryeh. *Power and Empowerment*. Philadelphia: Temple University Press, 1952.

Ballard, Edward Goodwin. *Man and Technology*. Pittsburgh: Duquesne University Press, 1988.

Berger, Peter, and Pullberg, Paul. "Reification and the Sociological Critique of Consciousness." *History and Theory* 4, 2 (1976): 202-210.

Bernard, Chester I. *The Functions of the Executive*. Cambridge, Mass.: Harvard University Press, 1938.

Bernstein, Paul. *Workplace Democratization*. New Brunswick, N.J.: Transaction Books, 1983.

Bish, Robert, and Ostrom, Vincent. *Understanding Urban Government*. Washington, D.C.: Domestic Affairs Study 20, American Enterprise Institute for Public Policy Research, 1973.

Blumberg, Paul. *Industrial Democracy: The Sociology of Participation*. New York: Schocken Books, 1968.

Boyte, Harry. *Commonwealth: A Return to Citizen Politics*. New York: The Free Press, 1989.

Bozeman, Barry. *All Organizations Are Public*. San Francisco: Jossey-Bass, 1987.

Brademas, John; Pierce, Neil; Richardson, Elliot; Ostrom, Vincent; and Weinberger, Caspar. "Organizational Rationality, Congressional Oversight and Decentralization: An Exchange." *Publius, the Journal of Federalism* 8 (1978): 111-119.

Buchanan, James M., and Tullock, Gordon. *The Calculus of Consent*. Ann Arbor: University of Michigan Press, 1974.

Calhoun, Craig, editor. *Habermas and the Public Sphere*. Cambridge, Mass.: The MIT Press, 1993.

Connolly, William. *Legitimacy and the State*. New York: New York University Press, 1984.

Dahl, Robert A. *A Preface to Economic Democracy*. Berkeley: University of California Press, 1985.

___. "The Science of Administration." *Public Administration Review* 7, 1 (1947): 1-11.

Davis, Charles R. "The Administrative Rational Model and Public Organization Theory." *Administration and Society* 28, 1 (May, 1996).

___. "A Critique of the Ideology of Efficency." *Humboldt Journal of Social Relations* 12, 2 (Spring-Summer, 1985): 73-85.

___. "Gulick's Efficiency: The Administrative Management View." *International Journal of Public Administration* 13, 2 (March, 1990): 603-619.

___. The Primacy of Self-Development in Chris Argyris' Writings," *International Journal of Public Administration* 10, 2 (1987): 177-207.

___. "Public Organizational Existence: A Critique of Individualism in Democratic Administration." *Polity* 22 (Spring, 1990): 397-418.

Denhardt, Robert B. *In the Shadow of Organization*. Lawrence: Regents Press of Kansas, 1981.

___. *The Pursuit of Significance & Strategies for Managerial Success in Public Organization*. Belmont, Calif.: Wadsworth Publishing Company, 1993.

___. *Theories of Public Organization*. 2nd ed. Belmont, Calif.: Wadsworth Publishing Company, 1993.

___. *Theories of Public Organization*. Monterey, Calif.: Brooks/Cole Publishing Company, 1984.

___, and Denhardt, Kathryn. "Public Administration and the Concept of Domination." *Administration and Society* 11, 1 (1979): 107-120.

Dewey, John. *The Public and Its Problems*. Athens, Ohio: Swallow Press, 1927.

Dunn, William N., and Fozouni, Bahman. *Toward a Critical Administrative Theory*. Administration and Policy Studies, No. 03-026. Beverly Hills: Sage Professional Paper, 1976.

Fay, Brian. *Social Theory and Political Practice*. London: George Allen & Unwin, 1975.

Fleron, Frederic, and Fleron, Lou Jean. "Administrative Theory as Repressive Political Theory." *Newsletter on Comparative Studies of Communism* 6 (1972): 3-47.

Golembiewski, Robert T. *Men, Management and Morality*. New York: McGraw Hill, 1965.

Greenburg, Edward. *Workplace Democracy: The Political Effects of Participation*. Ithaca: Cornell University Press, 1986.

Gulick, Luther. "Democracy and Administration Face the Future," *Public Administration Review* 37 (1977): 706-711.

___. "The Dynamics of Public Administration Today as Guidelines for the Future." *Public Administration Review* 43, 3 (May-June, 1983): 193-198.

___. "George Maxwell Had a Dream," In *American Public Administration: Past, Present, Future*, ed. Frederick C. Mosher, Tuscaloosa, Ala.: University of Alabama Press, 1975: pp. 255-257.

___. "Notes on the Theory of Organization," In *Papers on the Science of Administration*, ed. Luther Gulick and L. Urwick. New York: Institute of Public Administration, 1937: pp. 255-257.

___. "Politics, Administration, and the 'New Deal.'" *Annals of the American Academy of Political and Social Science* 169 (September, 1933): 55-66.

___. "Science, Values and Public Administration." In *Papers on the Science of Administration*, ed. Luther Gulick and L. Urwick. New York: Institute of Public Administration, 1937: 189-195.

Habermas, Jurgen. "The Public Sphere." *New German Critique* 1, 3 (1964): 49-55.

___. *Toward a Rational Society*. Boston: Beacon Press, 1970.

___. *The Structural Transformation of the Public Sphere: An Inquiry into a Category of Bourgeois Society* Cambridge, Mass.: MIT Press, 1989.

Harmon, Michael M. *Action Theory for Public Administration*. New York: Longman, 1981.

Hart, David K. and Scott, William G. "The Philosophy of American Management," *Southern Review of Public Administration* 6, 2 (Summer, 1982): 240-252.

Hohendal, Peter. "Jurgen Habermas: The Public Sphere." *New German Critique* 1, 3 (Fall, 1974): 45-48.

Horkheimer, Max. *Eclipse of Reason*. New York: Seabury Press, 1947.

Hummel, Ralph. *The Bureaucratic Experience*. 4th Ed. New York: St. Martin's Press, 1994.

Hunnius, Gerry, Garson, G. David, and Case, John. *Workers Control: A Reader on Labor and Social Change*. New York: Random House, 1973.

Ihara, Randall H. *Confronting the Problem of Political Vision: Gabriel Marcel, Emmanuel Mounier and Chris Argyris*. University of Tennessee, unpublished masters thesis. 1970.

Jacoby, Russell. *Social Amnesia: A Critique of Conformist Psychology from Adler to Laing*. Boston: Beacon Press, 1975.

Jaerisch, Ursula. "Max Weber's Contribution to the Sociology of Culture." In *Max Weber and Sociology Today*, ed. Otto Stamper. New York: Harper Torchbooks, 1971: pp. 221-239.

Jenkins, David. *Job Power: Blue and White Collar Democracy*. New York: Penguin 1974.

Kittel, Gerhard, editor. *Theological Dictionary of the New Testament*. Vol. 3 Grand Rapids, Mich.: William B. Eerdmans, 1965.

Lindberg, Leon N., editor. *The Energy Syndrome*. Lexington, Mass.: Lexington Books, 1977.

Loewith, Karl. "Weber's Interpretation of the Bourgeois-Capitalistic World in Terms of the Guiding Principle of 'Rationalization.'" In *Max Weber*, ed. Dennis Wrong. Englewood Cliffs, N.J.: Prentice Hall, 1970, pp.101-102.

Lonnroth, Mans. "Swedish Energy Policy: Technology in the Political Process," In Leon N. Linberg, ed., *The Energy Syndrome*. Lexington, Mass.: Lexington Books, 1977, pp. 255-283.

Lukacs, Georg. *History and Class Consciousness*. Cambridge, Mass.: MIT Press, 1971.

Lustig, R. Jeffrey. *Corporate Liberalism: The Origins of Modern American Political Theory, 1890-1920*. Berkeley: University of California Press, 1982.

March, James, and Simon, Herbert A. *Organizations*. New York: John Wiley and Sons, 1958.

Mommsen, Wolfgang. "Rationalization and Myth in Weber's Thought." In *The Political and Social Theory of Max Weber* (Chicago: University of Chicago Press, 1989), pp. 133-144.

Mosher, Frederick C., editor. *American Public Administration: Past, Present, Future*. Tuscaloosa, Ala.: The University of Alabama Press, 1975.

Nelkin, Dorothy. *Technological Decisions and Democracy: European Experiments in Public Participation*. Beverly Hills: Sage Publications, 1977.

Noble, David F. *America by Design: Science, Technology and the Rise of Corporate Capitalism*. New York: Alfred A. Knopf, 1979.

Ostrom, Vincent. "Artisanship and Artifact." *Public Administration Review* 40, 4 (1980): 309-317.

___. "Hobbes, Covenant, and Constitution," *Publius, the Journal of Federalism*. 10, 4 (1980): 83-100.

___. *The Intellectual Crisis in American Public Administration*, rev. ed. Tuscaloosa, Ala.: University of Alabama Press, 1989.

___.*The Political Theory of a Compound Republic: A Reconstruction of the Logical Foundations of American Democracy as Presented in The Federalist*. Blacksburg, Va.: Virginia Polytechnic Institute and State University, 1971.

___. *The Political Theory of a Compound Republic*. 2nd ed., Rev. and enlarged. Lincoln: University of Nebraska Press, 1987.

___. "Some Problems in Doing Political Theory: A Response to Golembiewski's 'Critique.'" *American Political Science Review* 7, 4 (1977): 1508-1525.

___. "The Undisciplinary Discipline of Public Administration: A Response to Stillman's Critique," *Publius, the Journal of Federalism* 6, 4 (1976), 304-307.

___, and Ostrom, Elinor. "Public Choice: A Different Approach to the Study of Public Administration." *Public Administration Review* 31 (March-April, 1971): 203-213.

___, Tiebout, Charles M., and Warren, Robert. "The Organization of Government in Metropolitan Areas: A Theoretical Inquiry." *American Political Science Review* 55 (1961): 831-842.

Pateman, Carole. *Participation and Democratic Theory*. Cambridge: Cambridge University Press, 1970.

Pranger, Robert J. *The Eclipse of Citizenship: Power and Participation in Contemporary Poltics*. New York: Holt, Rinehart and Winston, 1968.

Rainey, Hal. *Understanding and Managing Public Organizations*. San Francisco: Jossey-Bass, 1991.

Rasmussen, David M. "Between Autonomy and Sociality." *Cultural Hermeneutics* 1 (1973): 3-45.

Reich, Robert B. *The Next American Frontier*. New York: Penguin, 1983.

Reid, Herbert G., and Yanarella, Ernest J., "Critical Political Theory and Moral Development: Toward a Critical Phenomenological Outlook." University of Kentucky. Paper delivered at the Midwest Political Science Convention, April 30, 1976.

Riesenberg, Peter. *Citizenship In The Western Tradition*. Plato to Rousseau. Chapel Hill: University of North Carolina Press, 1992.

Scott, William G. *Chester Bernard and the Guardians of the Managerial State*. Lawrence: University of Kansas Press, 1992.

Simon, Herbert A. *Administrative Behavior*. 3rd ed. New York: The Free Press, 1976.

___. *Models of Man*. New York: Wiley, 1957

___. *Models of My Life*. New York: Basic Books, 1991.

___. "The Proverbs of Administration," *Public Administration Review* 6 (1946): 53-67.

___, Smithburg, Donald W., and Thompson, Victor A. *Public Administration*. New York: Harper & Row, 1950.

Skowronek, Stephen. *Building a New American State: The Expansion of National Administrative Capacities, 1877-1920*. Cambridge: Cambridge University Press, 1982.

Sullivan, William M. *Reconstructing Public Philosophy*. Berkeley: University of California Press, 1986.

Svara, James H. *Official Leadership in the City: Patterns of Conflict and Cooperation*. New York: Oxford University Press, 1990.

Thompson, Kirk. "Constitutional Theory and Political Action." *Journal of Politics* 31 (August, 1969): 655-681.

Thompson, Victor A. *Without Sympathy or Enthusiasm: The Problem of Administrative Compassion*. Tuscaloosa, Ala.: University of Alabama Press, 1975.

Tocqueville, Alexis de. *Democracy in America*. ed. and abridged by Richard Heffner. New York: Mentor Book, 1956.

Waldo, Dwight. *The Administrative State*, 2nd ed, New York: Holmes and Meier, Inc. 1984.

Waldo, Dwight. "Public Administration." *Journal of Politics* 30, 2 (May, 1968), p. 449.

Wamsley, Gary, Goodsell, Robert N., Kronenberg, Phillip J., Rohr, John A., et al. *Refounding Public Administration*. Newbury Park, Calif.: Sage Publications, 1990.

White, Leonard, *Introduction to Public Administration*, New York: Harper and Brothers, 1926.

Wisman, Jon D. "Legitimation, Ideology-Critique and Economics." *Social Research* 46 (Summer, 1976): 291-320.

Wolfe, Alan. *The Limits of Legitimacy*. New York: The Free Press, 1977.

Wolin, Sheldon S. *Politics and Vision: Continuity and Innovation in Western Political Thought*. Boston: Little, Brown and Company, 1960.

Yanarella, Ernest J., and Ihara, Randal H. "Environmental vs. Ecolo-
gical Perspectives on Acid Rain: The American Environmental
Movement and the West German Green Party." *The Acid Rain
Debate: Scientific, Economic and Political Dimensions*. Boulder,
Colo.: Westview Press, 1985. pp. 243-260.

Index

About the Author

CHARLES R. DAVIS is Associate Professor of Political Science at the University of Southern Mississippi. He holds the B.A. degree from the University of Louisville and the M.A. and Ph.D. from the University of Kentucky.

ISBN 0-275-95576-1

HARDCOVER BAR CODE